THE BUSES OF

HALIFAX
CORPORATION
&
JOINT OMNIBUS COMMITTEE
and their successors

Calderdale Joint Omnibus Committee : West Yorkshire PTE
Yorkshire Rider : First Calderline

David Bentley

An Autobus Review Publication

First published November 1998

ISBN 0 907834 41 8

Printed by Bakes & Lord Ltd.,
Beacon Road, Bradford BD6 3NB

AUTOBUS REVIEW PUBLICATIONS LTD.
42 Coniston Avenue, Queensbury,
Bradford, West Yorkshire BD13 2JD

INTRODUCTION

It is appropriate that in this the centenary year of the introduction of road public transport in Halifax, the tramway, the history of the bus operations of the local authority should have been recorded. Although the tramway history is not described in great detail, the major events pertaining to this type of traction are included particularly where it is affected by the developments resulting from the introduction of the new form of transport, the motor bus, between 1912 and 1939. The history of the bus undertaking goes into greater detail with the comprehensive recording of matters of routes, vehicles and the main personalities having an influence on the way the local authority bus operations developed in Halifax and its surrounding areas until their eventual demise on 31 March 1974. An overview is also given from this date of the operations which were taken over by the West Yorkshire Passenger Transport Executive and also the competition which ensued in the late 'eighties and 'nineties between its successor private operator CalderLine, part of the FirstGroup organisation, and the smaller bus undertakings springing up as a result of this move to deregulation. The book closes appropriately with a summary of the event that was organised to mark this the centenary of public transport in Halifax in 1998. It provides a fascinating history of the involvement of the local authority in municipal transport in Halifax and surrounding areas which has developed in a way that its founding fathers would not have imagined 100 years ago.

THE AUTHOR

My interest in public transport in the area developed with the daily journey to Northowram Primary School from 1945 on the pre-war AEC Regents, and later on the journey to Grammar School in Halifax on the AEC Regent IIIs and Daimlers in the 'fifties. In 1960 I became a conductor on the 48 Brighouse - Hebden Bridge through route at the time of the introduction of the 8ft. wide AEC Regent Vs, traffic inspector in 1963 and a traffic officer in 1966. Of particular interest at this time was the absorption of the Todmorden and Hebble undertakings into the Halifax fleet in the early 'seventies. I joined R.Travers Morgan 'The Bradford Bus Study' and then in 1975 the West Yorkshire County Council as a Traffic Engineer at Bishopgarth, Wakefield. In 1992 I became part of the 'major maintenance' team of the Department of Transport regional office in Leeds, which later became the Highways Agency, taking early retirement in October 1997 after serving in the Bridges and Design Build Finance Operate sections.

Whilst with Halifax Passenger Transport Department I qualified to become a Member of the Chartered Institute of Transport, and I am still proud to serve on the committee of the local Yorkshire Section of this professional body. I gained an M.Sc in Transport Planning and Engineering by taking a year's secondment from the County Council to Leeds University, attending the Institute for Transport Studies under the leadership of Professors Gwilliam and May. I was also a founder member of the Keighley Bus Museum in the early 'nineties.

ACKNOWLEDGEMENTS

Many people have encouraged me in turning my interest in the local public transport scene into the book you are reading now. In listing the many organisations, bodies and individuals who have helped me with their contribution, whether with information or photographs, I hope that no names have been missed and apolgise to anyone in the last category. I would like all to know that I am deeply indebted to them for all their help.

Grateful thanks are thus given to The PSV Circle for permission to quote from their comprehensive vehicles records; the staff of the public library reference section of the Halifax Courier for their help, particularly with the passenger transport minutes and summary of major events; and the Yorkshire Area Traffic Commissioner for reference to Notices and Proceedings. Particular mention must also be made of Donald Akrigg; Neil Cannon; Mrs.A.Greenwood; Nicholas Harris; Roy Marshall; John Sharp and Tim Worsnop who have all helped with the provision of photographs which have proved to be a valuable part of this fascinating history. Last, but not least, thanks must be extended to the publisher, Keith A. Jenkinson of Autobus Review Publications Ltd. who contributed much to the final chapter and whose assistance with the supporting information relating to the vehicles in the fleet has proved invaluable. The fact that this book has become a history of a century of public transport operation in the Halifax area and not just specifically covering the bus operating period from 1912 to 1974 is in no small measure due to his help and encouragement. Above all, he has been instrumental in helping me to achieve a lifetime's ambition - i.e. the recording of the local authority public transport scene in Halifax from its infancy to the present day for all posterity to enjoy, whether as a dedicated enthusiast or an interested layman. I have taken great pleasure in seeing this put into print and hope that likewise you will gain equally as much pleasure in its reading.

David Bentley M.Sc, M.C.I.T.
Northowram,
Halifax,
October 1998

THE EARLY YEARS

Municipal transport first began in Halifax on 29 June 1898 when the Corporation began operating electric trams on two routes from the town's General Post Office to Highroad Well and King Cross using ten open-top double deck cars which were painted in a blue and white livery and operated from a depot at Spring Hall, Pellon. This was three weeks later than originally planned, however, for although the initial inauguration had taken place on the fiftieth anniversary of the incorporation of the Borough on 9 June, the system was unable to open to passengers due to the essential Board of Trade inspection not having been carried out by that time. Running every ten minutes and with a flat 1d fare being charged (be it for an adult or child), the services were soon extended from the General Post Office to the Old Railway Station and in just over a year, a new depot was commissioned at Skircoat Road, this being opened in 1902. After extending its system and opening further routes upon which a high proportion of the track was situated on roads that were outside the Borough boundaries, a fact which did not please local ratepayers, the Corporation turned its attention towards other forms of public transport and as early as 1905 took the decision to purchase two 36-seat Milnes Daimler buses with which to commence a service to Mount Tabor. Before it could fulfil its plan, however, it found that it did not possess the necessary powers to operate them and thus the trams continued to reign supreme. Indeed it was not until 1911 that it first obtained Parliamentary consent to operate omnibuses within the Borough in connection with or in extension of its tramways, this being one of the provisions of the Halifax Corporation Act 1911. To this end after previously inspecting a motorbus on 12 June 1912 and travelling upon it to Ogden and then to Siddal on 21 September, members of the Halifax Corporation Tramways and Electricity Committee, led by its Chairman Charles Frederick Spencer, travelled in a motorbus over the routes of the proposed tramway extensions, taking in Elland, Brighouse, Rastrick, Huddersfield, Outlane, Stainland, Rishworth and Ripponden. The bus, a Daimler Silent Knight, was the property of Commercial Car Hirers Ltd., Cambridge Circus, London and had been brought to Halifax at the request of Councillor Spencer for this trial run. The Committee was highly delighted with its performance, reporting that 'it was silent running, flexible, almost free of vibration and those who travelled the whole distance in it on Saturday, probably 30 miles, felt at the finish as if they had been riding in a tramcar or an ordinary motor car the whole way'. Another trial trip was made by the tramway officials on the following day to Harrogate and back and they too were entirely satisfied with it. 'It has met with universal praise from all concerned' said Councillor Spencer. 'The upshot of this is that the Tramways and Electricity Committee will certainly recommend the adoption of a motorbus system in different parts. The Committee meet this afternoon on the question of motorbuses and we shall come to a definite decision on which routes to place them'. With this statement municipal bus operation in Halifax was born.

Accordingly the Tramways and Electricity Committee recommended the purchase from Commercial Car Hirers of a motorbus for the sum of £830 and an order was to be given for a further two additional motor omnibuses at a similar price. It was recommended that the motorbuses be run temporarily from Parkinson Lane via Pellon to Mount Tabor and that the fares for the conveyance of passengers should be as follows : From Pellon to Mount Tabor 1 1/2d and from Parkinson Lane to Pellon via Queens Road 1d and subject to the approval of the Board of Trade, the service be commenced, if practicable, on 14 October 1912.

The demonstration bus (a 22 hp CC-type Daimler) was one of the three to be purchased and was built with two compartments. It had seating for 28 passengers but with those standing could carry 40 people. Its bodywork was by Commercial Car Hirers who agreed to build the remaining 2 buses to meet the requirements of the district in which they were to operate.

The approval of the Town Council meeting the following week was not without dissent, however, the main objection being that although they knew that motorbuses had been successful in London where there were level streets, conditions were completely dissimilar in Halifax with its mostly hilly terrain and that the trial had not been long enough to properly test the vehicle's efficiency. Motorbuses were still in their experimental stage and it was felt that it would be preferable to give a thorough trial to one bus before committing themselves to a further purchase. However, the argument for three buses won the day as it was intended to use two of them on the Mount Tabor and Siddal routes with the third being on standby for use for duplication purposes. If the buses did not come up to expectation on the routes upon which they were to be placed, they could easily be taken off with only a small capital outlay. Although it was expected that the buses would lose money in the initial years, the minute of the Committee was adopted by a large majority of the Town Council, thus setting into motion, with vision and foresight, municipal bus operation in Halifax which was to develop and expand in ways which could not have originally been foreseen at this time over a period of almost 62 years.

The inauguration of the first municipal motorbus service in the town took place on Wednesday 16 October 1912 amid much rejoicing at the Mount Tabor end of the route. Members of the Tramways and Electricity Committee with other invited members of the Council travelled to Mount Tabor via Queens Road and Pellon from the Rook Inn, Hanson Lane, thus traversing the route upon which the vehicle was to run. On arriving at Mount Tabor the bus and its passengers were cordially cheered by the local

Posed outside the New Inn at Mount Tabor on its inaugural journey from Halifax on 16 October 1912 is Commercial Car Hirers-bodied Daimler CC-type no.1 which carries its original registration mark A.I.D.Y.
Courtesy of A.Wilson

Halifax Corporation's first motor omnibus, Daimler CC-type no.1 (CP272) forms the backdrop for this group of officials at Skircoat Road depot circa 1913. Fitted with a centre entrance Commercial Car Hirers body, it carried its destination details of roof-mounted blocks which could be revolved according to the terminus it served. *R.Needham collection*

inhabitants who had mustered in considerable numbers, despite the inclement weather, to welcome the inauguration. The members of the Council, together with representatives of the district, were then entertained by the Tramways and Electricity Committee to tea at the New Inn. The assembled party was told that if they showed their appreciation of the bus by placing plenty of fares in the conductor's hands, the Committee, at no distant date, would take cognisance of the fact that this route needed some other form of traction. They had got a vehicle which would be a credit to the department and when the time came that they had to consider other routes for motor traction, if it turned out to be a success, their purchases would not stop at 3 buses. If it was

shown that they ran as well as tramways at a similar cost without the capital outlay then they would be prepared to consider other districts which required motorbuses.

Whilst the Councillors and guests were at tea, the driver took a party of schoolchildren from the district to Halifax and back and quite a few heads were turned on Commercial Street at the sound of youthful elation emanating from the new bus. On the same day as the official inauguration, an order was given to Commercial Car Hirers for the supply of the 2 further motorbuses at a cost not exceeding £830 each as well as instructions to partition a portion of the tram depot at Skircoat Road for heating apparatus and the housing of the motorbuses at an estimated cost of £50.

Fitted with solid rubber tyres and showing the steps leading to its rear entrance, blue liveried Daimler CC-type motorbus no.2 (CP281) stands at Jubilee Road top, Siddal in 1913. Its driver (Frank Evans) and conductor (Jeramy Thornton) whose ticket punch clearly seen appear to be very proud of their new charge.
Courtesy of A.Greenwood

Obviously creating a large amount of interest, Daimler CC-type 2 (CP281) and 3 (CP284) stand at Mount Tabor in 1913 soon after their entry into service. Both are painted in the Corporation's blue livery and carry Commercial Car Hirers bodywork with a rear platform and entrance.
Courtesy of A.Wilson

The first day, Thursday 17 October, upon which the new motorbus ran between Hanson Lane and Mount Tabor resulted in an income of £4.11.3 representing 13d per bus mile, a figure which was thought to be exceedingly satisfactory. Two months later, at the end of December, on Mondays to Thursdays the service on the Queens Road section between the Rook and Pellon was discontinued between 8.00am and 2.00pm (although a full day's service was still maintained on Fridays and Saturdays) and additionally a timetable was prepared for a new motorbus service which was to commence in the second week of January of the following year operating between Alexandra Street, Church Street and Water Lane to Ashgrove Avenue, Siddal with a maximum 1 1/2d fare with facilities for 1d return tickets to Siddal at the transfer stage of Cross Keys Inn. Objections were made to the use of Water Lane on account of its gradient being a severe test for the vehicle and driver, but despite these reservations the service began on Monday 13 January 1913 on a route which had now been extended to a terminus near Siddal school at Cinderhills. The weather conditions and the state of the roads were as trying for a motor omnibus as could be imagined, but nevertheless Water Lane and the snow covered roads were negotiated without any major problem. Before the return journey for the officials taking part, tea was taken in the Wesleyan schoolroom while the bus was used to provide free transport to and from Halifax town centre for children and their mothers, a privilege that was eagerly taken advantage of. The success of the service can be judged by the fact that, despite the first bus not taking up its duties before 8.15am, during the first week of operation 4,766 passengers were carried and the mileage earnings exceeded those of any of the tram sections (14.22d per bus mile as opposed to the highest earning tram section, West End, producing 13.09d per car mile).

The three Daimlers were all of the CC-type fitted with Silent Knight 4-cylinder sleeve valve petrol engines, 4-speed chain driven gearbox, Ferodo-lined cone clutch, worm final drive and solid tyres on cast steel wheels. Given fleet numbers 1-3, they were originally registered A1DY, A2DY and A3DY, painted in a blue livery, and featured a rear passenger door reached by two steps and an open rear platform surrounded by a rail fence.

On 20 January 1913 the Mount Tabor bus reverted to its former timetable and despite having a total deficiency, year ending 31 March 1913, of £329 including the garage and initial costs of motorbus operation, the service was extended on 4 April from Mount Tabor to Wainstalls and two months later the return journey commenced to be operated via Balkram Edge for a trial period. Wakes Week in July 1913 witnessed the arrival of the first double deck bus in the town following arrangements having been made with the Daimler company to operate one of its vehicles on trial on one of the motorbus routes with Daimler additionally supplying the petrol and the driver and the Corporation providing the conductor and paying Daimler 6d per mile. Soon after its arrival the bus was placed on the Wainstalls route which was well patronised with holidaymakers going to Withins and Ogden before returning by tram from Causeway Foot. It was not, however, operated via Balkram Edge as this deviation had been withdrawn

before the double decker's arrival. At this same time the Siddal route was altered to operate via New Road instead of Horton Street and Church Street. The Corporation's new bus services were, by now, proving reliable and in their second year of operation the three Daimlers ran some 34.025 miles and turned in a profit of £259, thus reversing the deficit of the previous twelve months.

The outbreak of hostilities on 4 August 1914 affected the undertaking in an unusual way. As a result of the war Liga Tyres Ltd., a company formed for importing German made tyres and controlled by the enemy had gone into liquidation leaving the Corporation to find a new source of supply for its small motorbus fleet. Shortly afterwards the Tramways and Electricity Committee decided to promote another Parliamentary Bill and asked Stainland District Council if they wished to enter into an agreement which, if a motorbus service paid its way, would result in the laying of a tram track within five years in return for an initial subsidy against losses. At a special meeting of the Town Council, the Bill was endorsed despite Stainland refusing to guarantee a subsidy in view of recent approaches by Huddersfield Corporation. The provisions relating to motorbuses were :

(a) to authorise the Corporation to run motorbuses along streets within the Borough or along any street forming through routes or connecting other streets within the Borough.

(b) to confirm agreements made or to be made within local authorities, or some of them, in respect of motor omnibuses in their districts.

(c) to authorise the Corporation to construct, maintain, equip and work trolley vehicles within the Borough from Spring Hall Lane to Mount Tabor and Wainstalls, and from Skircoat Road to Siddal via Hunger Hill.

(d) to enable the Corporation to run motor omnibuses outside the Borough.

Trolley vehicles were proposed in view of the difficulties the committee had had in making the omnibuses pay whilst a previous agreement made with the Mytholmroyd District Council was revised to allow for a reduction in subsidy in view of the conditions attached to its previous consent in allowing trams to run through Mytholmroyd which provided for an extension to Cragg Vale.

The Parliamentary Bill was approved at a public meeting at Ebenezer School on 18 January 1915 when it was stated that if the Town Council removed the Cragg Vale motorbus from the Bill, the Corporation would lose the lease of the Mytholmroyd tramway after thirty one years. There was no demand for a poll of ratepayers by opponents despite Halifax having to pay 3/8d per mile to the District Councils or to the West Riding Authority towards the cost of roads over which motorbuses would run. Approval was duly given by the House of Lords on 22 April 1915 following certain adjustments, although all the provisions relating to bus and trolleybus operation were passed and thus the Halifax Corporation Act 1915 became law on 25 June. This meant that the Corporation could now run motorbuses anywhere within the Borough as well as from Triangle to Ripponden and Mytholmroyd to Cragg Vale and, subject to the consent of the Board of Trade

Surprisingly, three new buses were delivered to the Corporation in 1916 during the midst of World War I. Daimler Y-types with bodies built in the Skircoat Road workshops, they were used as replacements for the undertaking's original three buses. No.5 (CP747), seen here at Savile Park Moor, gave eleven years service before being sold in 1927 to North Western Road Car Co. Ltd.
R.Marshall collection

Seen in 1918 after having a gas holder fitted on its roof to allow it to be operated on town gas, Daimler Y-type 5 (CP747) is seen with its driver and conductor at a location which has been unable to be determined. *R.Marshall collection*

and the local and road authorities, along any other route outside the Borough as well as gaining the power to borrow £58,370 for the purchase of motorbuses and the extension of Skircoat Road tram depot.

On 30 March 1916 a tender submitted by the Daimler Company for the supply of 2 Y-type chassis, later increased to 3, was accepted as replacements for the original trio of CC-type buses. Numbered 4-6, these were fitted with 23-seat rear entrance bodies built by the Corporation in its own workshops and all entered service at the start of July, replacing the three original buses whose bodies were then removed prior to their chassis being sold to the British Automobile Traction Company. When in 1921 all motor vehicles were required to carry registration numbers, they were given identities CP742, CP747 and CP748. Because of difficulties in obtaining petrol supplies, however, in 1917 the motorbus service to Siddal was put onto part day operation and the complete closure of the Wainstalls section was only prevented by the conversion of bus no.5 to run on town gas at an estimated cost of £76. The gasholder, of which four were purchased, was mounted on the roof of the bus and on more than one occasion it was known to have been blown off whilst operating on the windy Wainstalls route.

As a result of the continuing uncertainty of petrol supplies, on 19 November 1917 the Tramways and Electricity Committee took the decision to purchase 2 Railless trolleybuses from Dundee Corporation at a cost of £625 each, but this brought objections from the Finance Committee on the grounds of the cost of ancillary equipment and damage to the roads. In its defense, the Tramways and Electricity Committee stated that no special wires were to be erected off the route as, by the introduction of accumulators, it was possible to operate them four or five miles beyond the tramways without wires. Their restricted pay load would enable savings to be made in highway maintenance and the total cost of petrol driven vehicles was three times the amount of the railless buses as well as serving the national interest better.

Sanction for the purchase was given by a huge majority at the meeting of the Town Council on 5 December 1917. Arriving in Halifax in January 1918, surprisingly neither of the railless vehicles were placed in passenger service and instead one was used as a meals kitchen, the other at first as an Army recruiting office and later as a mobile cash office, although ostensibly it had been the intention to use them as lorries to run a parcels service to Bradford!

With peace having now returned, the purchase of four more buses was contemplated together with the acquisition of a new tower wagon. Although the former failed to materialise, the tower wagon did, based on an AEC YC-type chassis at a cost of £1006. This took up its duties in June 1919, although as will be seen later, it was soon put to a different use. Meanwhile, a meeting of Mytholmroyd District Council with the Tramways and Electricity Committee on 23 February 1920 resulted in the proposal to put one bus on the Mytholmroyd to Cragg Vale route between the County Bridge and Church Bank between 10.0am and 10.0pm on an hourly basis with the bus running light between Halifax and Mytholmroyd. The picturesque Cragg Valley running practically at right angles to Calder Dale from the thriving village of Mytholmroyd was on Saturday 3 April a centre of unusual activity and interest when the first Corporation bus arrived to open the new service which had initially been proposed before the war began. However, the operation was largely on a trial basis with Halifax retaining the right to cease running should there be a financial loss over and above the £20 already available as subsidy. Although there was nothing in the nature of a civic opening of the route, a crowd of village folk gathered round to watch the bus (No.6) arrive promptly and take up its position on the spare ground outside the Dusty Miller Inn. There was a rush for seats with all concerned being anxious to have the privilege of 'going up' on the first trip on the 'Cragg Vale Chariot' and the bus set off with a capacity load, but unfortunately without the presence of a single local councillor. Despite this, however, after operating for less than a month the new service proved not to be a successful financial venture and as a result the fares were increased by 100% on 28 April coupled with a curtailment to afternoon and evening operation only. This too proved to be a disappointment and with all the subsidy being absorbed, the last journey was undertaken on 28 May after which the bus was then transferred to the Wainstalls route for the Whitsuntide period. Another operator, Mr.F.A.Clarke, took over on the following day including an early morning workmen's bus but this too was comparatively short lived and lasted only until the end of 1920 when its owner decided to emigrate to South Africa on health grounds. Mytholmroyd District Council rejected operating its own vehicles on the grounds of the cost of obtaining a Parliamentary order and Todmorden Corporation was prevented from running

Commercial Car Hirers-bodied Daimler CC-type 3 (CP284) appeared to be carrying mainly men when photographed on a journey from Mount Tabor to Halifax, although a lady and child are also visible amongst the bowler hatted and flat capped passengers. *R.Needham collection*

the service due to its lack of statutory powers for that area and thus Mytholmroyd was once again without a bus service.

On 7 January 1921 the Chairman of the Tramways and Electricity Committee, Alderman Alan Fawcett, resigned because of the failure of Halifax Town Council to endorse the Committee's appointment of the Tramways Engineer J.D.Galloway as General Tramways Manager. Meanwhile, Traffic Manager James D.Caird because of his continued ill health was given three months notice

to terminate his employment and on 20 May 1921 Ben Hall who had been General Manager and Engineer of Wigan Corporation Tramways took up the appointment of General Tramways Manager at Halifax in readiness for the next major step in the history of the undertaking, the Wainstalls railless traction route. One of the first moves made by Ben Hall, however, was to alter the livery of Halifax's trams and buses from blue to red, the latter being the colour used by Wigan Corporation from where he came.

TROLLEYBUSES & MORE BUSES

Having been used in non passenger carrying roles since their purchase at the beginning of 1918 it was now thought that the time had come to experiment with the two former Dundee 'Stouries' trackless vehicles and to this end it was decided to electrify the existing motorbus route between Pellon and Wainstalls. A tender for the erection of overhead equipment was accepted in October 1919 at a price of £6390 while the two railless vehicles, which had been built in 1912 and were fitted with 25-seat Milnes Voss bodies, were taken into the Corporation's Skircoat Road workshops to undergo renovation. After a Ministry of Transport recommendation that the route should be widened at certain parts and the condition of the road improved, the route was opened without any blaze of publicity on 21 July 1921 with a fare of 4d for the complete journey with other ordinary and transfer stages in between. However, motorbuses were still used, particularly in the early morning, and permission was given to charge the same fares. The transfer system was soon abolished and on 14 December was replaced with penny stages on both this and the Siddal route.

Meanwhile, in an unusual move during the late summer of 1921, the Corporation's two-year old AEC YC-type tower wagon

(CP93) was taken into the Skircoat Road workshops and fitted with a new home built front entrance 24-seat single deck bus body which was suitable for one person operation, emerging in its new form in September of that year and to take its place in the ancillary fleet, Daimler Y-type bus no.6 (CP748) was removed from service and given the tower wagon body previously fitted to the AEC. Earlier in the year as a result of new vehicle registration regulations, the two railless vehicles had to comply and became CP2020 and CP2021 in April and May respectively.

Following a request from residents in the Wheatley area to the north-west of Halifax, a distance of two miles, a limited motorbus service was started on 2 June 1922 from Crossley Street to a terminus at Page Hill. This was operated by a new Dennis 50-cwt bus fitted with 24-seat front entrance bodywork built by the Corporation. Given fleet number 7 and designed for one person operation, it broke new ground in the town by being the first bus owned by the Corporation to be fitted with pneumatic tyres. As well as giving a better ride, due to having 'pump-up' tyres it effected a saving of £12 per annum on its road fund licence. In the meantime, following an experiment with one man operation on the Siddal route, despite complaints of timekeeping

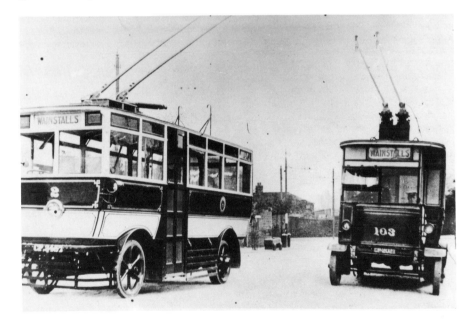

Two of the Corporation's three trolleybuses pose for the photographer in the late summer of 1924. No.2 (CP3457) on the left is a Tilling Stevens with Corporation-built bodywork which was but a couple of months old while on the right is 103 (CP2021), one of a pair of Railless vehicles purchased from Dundee Corporation six years earlier. *R.Marshall collection*

Starting life as a tower wagon in 1919, AEC YC-type 6 (CP93) was fitted with a Corporation-built 24-seat bus body in September 1921 and gave four years service before being withdrawn in July 1926. Although its chassis was then used as a salvage wagon, its body survived until 1931 in use as a bus shelter. *D.Akrigg collection*

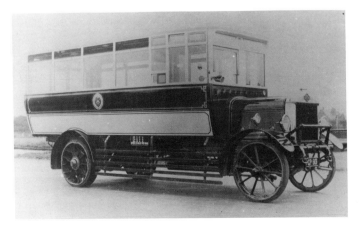

unreliability, the Corporation saw this as a means of reducing costs and thus converted all its services to this mode of operation during August. In connection with this, the two remaining Y-type Daimlers were rebuilt from rear to front entrance layout to make them suitable for one manning.

Until now, the bus fleet had really been an insignificant part of the Tramways Department, but the world was about to change. The first inclination of what was to come materialised when a Mr.Bateson began to run a bus service from Ripponden into Sowerby Bridge over the Triangle tram route. The Tramways and Electricity Committee was understandably aggrieved by this and indicated in December 1922 that if he persisted it would use its current powers and introduce a competitive bus service. Mr.Bateson took the hint and ceased his operation.

Although a comparatively uneventful year in terms of operations, 1923 witnessed the arrival of a further Dennis 50-cwt

single decker which, like its predecessor, was fitted with a 24-seat front entrance body built in the Corporations own workshops at Skircoat Road. Numbered 8 (CP3037) it was placed in service in July to provide the undertaking with a fifth bus. During the following year the railless fleet was also increased in size when a new Tilling Stevens RC2 chassis was purchased at a cost of £763 and fitted with a 26-seat front entrance body built by the Corporation. Like the motorbuses it was equipped for one person operation and in June it joined the two former Dundee vehicles on the solitary service to Wainstalls.

In September 1924 a conference held between Halifax and its neighbouring authorities to consider the question of motor omnibuses proved that they were alive to the possibilities of this form of transport and it was hoped that Halifax would keep abreast of development. It was stated that 'the motorbus is knocking vigorously at our doors as it were, and if prompt steps are not taken, private firms will be competing on the Halifax tram routes in several directions. Motorbus companies in Lancashire were already casting their eyes towards Ripponden with a view to running a service to link up with the Halifax tramways. In welcoming motorbuses the outside authority was not likely to consider the feelings of Halifax if they were to benefit from the invasion'.

Following permission being given by both Elland and Sowerby District Councils, a new motorbus service was introduced between Hollins Mill Lane, Sowerby Bridge and the Royal Hotel, Elland on 10 November 1924 which travelled along Wakefield Road through Copley. On this, the through fare charged was 4 1/2d and transfer tickets were issued to allow passengers to reach Halifax by tramcar from Copley and Elland by changing at Wakefield Road end.

After being refused licences to operate between Sowerby Bridge and Elland, Halifax and Huddersfield via lland, and a local Queens Road service, Halifax independent O. & C. Holdsworth took the law into its own hands by putting on a service with 3 Leyland A13-type single deck buses serving an area covering Brighouse, Southowram, Halifax, Holmfield, Denholme, Cullingworth and Bingley on 1 December 1924. The greater part of this route was not covered by tramways and a parking place was obtained in Halifax town centre on land opposite the Victoria Hall at the side of the Palace Theatre for picking up outward-bound passengers. There was to be no picking up in the Halifax area on inward journeys but passengers were able to be set down at any point and there seemed to be no doubt that the new service was going to be a great boon to a large population badly situated with respect to transport facilities. In response, on 15 December the Tramways and Electricity Committee took the unprecedented step of adding a further 6 Dennis 50-cwt buses to its existing order for 2 without having any definite plans for their route allocation and additionally instituted legal proceedings against O. & C. Holdsworth for inaugurating its service without a licence. The charges were dealt with by the magistrates on 31 December 1924 and to two of them Holdsworth's pleaded guilty, stating that they had offended under a misapprehension, believing that a licence was being granted to them by the local authority. Although these charges were dismissed, to six others they pleaded not guilty, claiming that having resorted to pre-booking at their parking ground they had kept within the law, a fact which the Corporation disputed. The magistrates imposed a fine of £1 in each case but allowed an appeal, and thus the service continued.

In February 1925 the Sowerby Bridge to Elland service was extended in Elland from the Royal Hotel to the Town Hall, this

change taking place about the same time that O. & C. Holdsworth started another illegal service between Halifax and Huddersfield via Elland. Following a public meeting protesting against the refusal by the Corporation to grant a licence to O. & C. Holdsworth for a service to Bradshaw which would be of great benefit to its residents, the Corporation was asked to provide such a service or that of Holdsworths would continue. The Town Council finally yielded to this pressure and a service began on 18 February 1925 to a point near Bradshaw Church, running on the same route as the Holdsworth's Bingley service within the Borough. It was operated by the first of the 8 new Dennis buses (9-16 : CP3810-5 & CP3905/6), all of which had entered service by March with the first six having Strachan & Brown bodywork and the remaining two, bodies built by the Corporation in its Skircoat Road workshops. All these wore the Corporation's livery of red with a cream roof, window surrounds and skirt panels, suitably lined of course, and carried the Halifax coat of arms centrally on each side.

Prior to the inauguration of the Bradshaw route, O. & C. Holdsworth had on 26 January 1925 started yet another illegal service, this time from Halifax to Greetland while three days later West Vale Garage Company extended its established service from Stainland to Outlane to start at Holywell Green in competition with the Corporation's tramcar route which operated as far as Stainland. On 13 February, O. & C. Holdsworth once again found itself facing Halifax's magistrates when it appeared before them on a charge of unlawfully permitting unlicensed hackney carriages to ply for hire in the Borough. Once more, a fine was imposed on the company! Less than a week later, however, Mytholmroyd District Council granted Holdsworths a

Showing Halifax and Rochdale in their destination apertures, Hall Lewis-bodied Karrier CL4s 24 & 25 (CP5226 & CP5227) are seen here when new in October 1926 prior to being fitted with their registration plates. *R.Marshall collection*

licence, subject to satisfactory fares and stopping places while on 17 March an enquiry was held by the Ministry of Transport at Halifax Town Hall as a result of the appeal by Holdsworths in respect of its application for licences to run omnibuses through Halifax to districts beyond. The services under discussion were :

Route 1. Halifax - Salterhebble - Greetland - Wall Nook - Barkisland.
Route 2. Halifax - King Cross - Triangle - Ripponden.
Route 3. Halifax - King Cross - Tuel Lane - Hebden Bridge.
Route 4. Halifax via alternative routes - Highroad Well - Warley.
Route 5. Halifax - Ovenden Cross - Causeway Foot - Bingley.
Route 6. Halifax - Southowram - Brighouse.
Route 7. Halifax - Elland - Huddersfield.

While the appeal relating to routes 2, 3 and 4 was disallowed, the Ministry stated that it was of the opinion that the Corporation should grant licences for routes 1, 5 and 6 provided that Holdsworths gave an undertaking to arrange their fares with a view to discouraging their buses being used for short journeys along the tram routes. In respect of route 7, the Ministry considered that the Corporation should grant a licence on receipt from Holdsworths of an undertaking to arrange their fares with a view to discouraging the use of their vehicles between any two points over the part of the route which was served by the tramway of Halifax Corporation and in the event of Halifax and/or Huddersfield Corporation operating an omnibus service over this route, the licensing authority should not seek to impose upon Holdsworths terms or conditions more onerous than those under which the omnibus services on this route are operated by either or both municipal authorities. Halifax Corporation responded by commencing jointly with Huddersfield Corporation a through service of motorbuses on 22 August 1925 and timetables were drawn up to prevent overlapping by either the Corporations or O. & C. Holdsworth vehicles.

In the meantime, on 6 May an extension of the service to Bradshaw took place to a point around half a mile through Bradshaw village whilst on the same day the Siddal service was extended through Halifax to King Cross via the Boulevards and Haugh Shaw Road. By this time the influx of new motorbuses necessitated the erection of a special garage and permission was given for this to be constructed at the northern end of the Skircoat Road tram depot.

A month prior to the arrival of 4 more Dennis 50-cwt buses (17-20 : CP4397-400), all of which were fitted with bodies built by the Corporation, a service from the Old Station to Warley via Fountain Street, Hopwood Lane, Warley Road and Highroad Well was started on 21 September 1925 while an Inner Circle route serving Pellon Lane, Hanson Lane, Queens Road and Parkinson Lane in both directions from a terminus at Southgate commenced on 9 November. Finally, early in December, and without the necessary authority, O. & C. Holdsworth started to operate between Halifax and the Travellers Rest near Midgley via Luddenden Foot, illustrating once again the company's disregard for the law.

After a quiet start, 1926 got under way when at the end of March the Bradshaw service was further extended to terminate at Pitt Hill and around this same time Ben Hall tendered his resignation after accepting the appointment of General Manager and Engineer of Portsmouth Corporation. On 12 April his replacement, Walter Theodore Young who had been General

Manager and Engineer of Dundee Corporation, was appointed and ultimately took up his new position on 5 July. Meanwhile the advent of the General Strike on 3 May left the Corporation able only to run a skeleton service of trams which were confined to the first stages from the centre of the town. These were supplemented by motorbuses of the Corporation and those of a number of independent operators who largely covered the out-districts for a few days until the difficulties were able to be resolved.

Since Ryburn Garage and Transport Company had been operating for some time between Rishworth and Halifax without a licence, the Town Council on 5 May gave authorisation for the necessary action to be taken against this independent concern as well as informing the Watch Committee of the increasing number of motorbus services and growing competition by private companies which was being introduced or threatened, to ensure that there were no illegalities in their operation.

In July 1926 a further 3 Strachan & Brown-bodied Dennis 50-cwt single deck buses (21-3 : CP4987-9) were received and placed in service and approval was given for a new service between Halifax, Pellon, Mount Tabor, Mixenden and Illingworth which gave Walter Young, who was no great lover of railless traction and had indeed been responsible for its demise in Dundee, the opportunity to discontinue the trackless service on the Wainstalls section. This was achieved on 31 October and on the following day motorbuses were substituted and the town centre terminus was altered to Cow Green. Following their withdrawal, two of the trolleybuses were scrapped by the Corporation whilst the third (one of the ex.Dundee vehicles) became a permanent way site office and was parked on the depot forecourt until around 1942. Also taken out of service were the two remaining Daimler CC-type buses, the bodies of which were

The conductor of Hall Lewis-bodied Karrier CL4 26 (CP5228) proudly poses in front of his charge during a journey from Halifax to Rochdale. *K.A.Jenkinson collection*

removed by the Corporation and used as shelters at Illingworth and Mount Tabor whilst their chassis were sold to the Regent Distribution Company of London who quickly resold them to North Western Road Car Co. of Stockport who fitted them with secondhand Birch bodies and placed them in service.

Late in 1926 a 3-axle Karrier CY6 bus (CX8989) powered by a Dorman 4JU engine and fitted with Hall Lewis 25-seat front entrance bodywork was borrowed by the Corporation from its manufacturer for trials on various of its services. Painted in a bright red livery it became known as the 'red lettuce' and soon became a familiar sight around Halifax and its suburbs. Obviously keen to support local industry (although Karriers were built in Huddersfield rather than Halifax), an order was immediately placed with Karrier for 6 CL4-type chassis which were to be fitted with 26-seat front entrance Hall Lewis bodies suitable for one person operation. These (24-9 : CP5226-31) duly arrived in October and generated a further order for Karrier chassis, this being for 12 CL6s fitted with Dorman 6-cylinder petrol engines for delivery in 1927.

On 27 August the linking of Halifax with Rochdale finally took place. Soyland District Council had previously withheld its consent to pick up passengers in its area until Halifax made concessions with the last bus and fare stages in its territory. However, an enquiry was held by the Ministry of Transport on 4 October 1926 into the question of the right to operate their own bus services being granted to Halifax Corporation for routes to Rochdale as well as Cleckheaton. Objections came from the LMS Railway Company, Ryburn Garage and Transport Company, O. & C. Holdsworth and the Commercial Users Association, although at this stage it was not opposed by West Riding County Council. At the end of November notification was received from the Minister that he was not satisfied that a sufficient case had been made out to justify consent for the Rochdale service, although powers were granted for that to Cleckheaton. The Corporation immediately reapplied for the licence to run to Rochdale and the service continued to operate in the meantime. On 1 February 1927 Soyland District Council gave its consent also to Ryburn

placed in service (1-5 : CP5734-8) with the sixth (6 : CP5739) following a month later although these were not without their troubles and it was quickly reported that they were using a great deal of engine oil, blowing cylinder head gaskets, poor starters and suffered from fuel starvation, particularly on the arduous Rochdale route. Despite this, however, the Karrier CY6 demonstrator which had been continuously used by the Corporation since new was purchased at around this same time and was given fleet number 30.

Controversy still surrounded the Rochdale service and on 20 July 1927 West Riding County Council authorised its Law and Parliamentary Committee to take all necessary steps to obtain an injunction or order to restrain Halifax Corporation from running omnibuses from Halifax to Rochdale without the consent of the County Council as required by Section 15 of the Halifax Corporation Act of 1915. If the Corporation continued to act in opposition to the established law, an injunction would be applied for. Two weeks later the Corporation retorted by asking the Town Clerk to take all the necessary action to defend any proceedings which the West Riding County Council might think fit to institute against it. And so the battle continued! On the third day of the following month the Tramways General Manager was given permission to run a service of motorbuses on the following routes
(a) Cragg Vale, Hebden Bridge and Heptonstall.
(b) Hebden Bridge, Blackshaw Head and Widdop Gate.
(c) Luddenden and Luddenden Foot.

Services to Luddenden and Widdop Gate commenced on the following day (4 August) and what had been regarded as a wild dream not many years ago of providing remote places that had until recently never been served by any form of public transport with a link to its nearest town became reality. On 5 August, Hebble Bus Services responded to the challenge by extending its service to Midgley Post Office from Luddenden but immediately Luddenden Foot District Council deprecated the dog-in-a-manger attitude of Halifax Corporation and set up a conference on 22 September with representatives from other affected authorities to discuss the refusal of the Corporation to license Hebble's buses

One of six Karrier WL6 buses purchased new in 1928 and fitted with Harris & Hassall 32-seat dual-door bodywork, 46 (CP6928) like its sisters was suitable for one-man-operation.
R.Needham collection

Garage and Transport Company to operate services between Halifax and Rochdale and Halifax and Oldham, subject to satisfactory timetables being maintained and additionally the company was requested to run in co-operation with other omnibus services in the district. Meanwhile, Oldham Corporation had begun an hourly service into Halifax and a joint service could well have been introduced had it not been for the attitude of the West Riding County Council. On 7 March 1927 the Calder Valley saw the introduction of its first through bus to Halifax when O. & C. Holdsworth, who now traded as Hebble Bus Services, began a regular service from Halifax to Hebden Bridge and Heptonstall, having previously only run between Hebden Bridge and Luddenden Foot. Owing to the steep gradient, however, it had to operate via Cross Lane, Whitehall Nook and Slack Bottom to the centre of Heptonstall village and charged different fares for the up and down journeys!

On 5 June 1927 the first 5 of the new Karrier CL6s were

plying between Halifax and Luddenden. Passengers were only allowed to board the bus in Halifax if they were in possession of a return ticket and the Council felt that neither Halifax or anyone else should have a monopoly. Mytholmroyd already insisted that the licence restrictions should be removed from the Hebble operations before granting a licence for Halifax to run between Mytholmroyd and Hebden Bridge and a petition was received from Cragg Vale requesting the Council to take all reasonable steps to restrain Halifax Corporation from running in that area between Bridge End, Mytholmroyd and Turvin, Cragg Vale since an adequate service was already being provided by private enterprise. Despite this, a service to Cragg Vale commenced on 12 September whilst also on this same date a petition was received by Midgley District Council against the running by Halifax Corporation from 26 August of buses in competition with Hebble Bus Services. It transpired that the Corporation had started the service between the bottom of Luddenden Lane and

Mytholmroyd via Scout Head without notifying the Council and with approximately 100 buses per day running along Luddenden Lane, the Council was becoming concerned about the road deterioration being caused by such an unnecessary service. Until Halifax Corporation agreed to licence the buses of the Hebble company, Midgley residents were asked to boycott the Corporation buses.

An agreement for the first takeover by the Corporation of a competing operator was reached when Ryburn Garage and Transport Company of Sowerby Bridge agreed to sell its business to the municipal undertaking for the sum of £9000 with effect from 1 November 1927. Included in the deal were 6 Karrier single deck buses which nicely fitted in to the Corporation fleet, various other equipment and spares and three services : Halifax to Sowerby (Steep Lane); Halifax to Rishworth and Halifax to Ripponden (White Hart). As was to be expected, the purchase was subject to an undertaking from Ryburn Garage not to engage in any business in competition with the trams or motorbuses of the Corporation. Within days of the takeover, however, a complaint was received by the Corporation from Rishworth District Council that the fares previously charged had been increased and that the timetable had been altered and was not of equivalent advantage to the inhabitants as it had formerly been, as well as pointing out that no official request for licences had been made to the Council.

Before any of these complaints could be addressed, on 21 November, as expected, Halifax Town Council received a writ and statement of claim by West Riding County Council applying for an injunction against the Corporation running motorbuses between Halifax and Rochdale without the consent of the County Council and the Ministry of Transport. When the order was made for the injunction in the Chancery Division on 27 February 1928, Rochdale Corporation, who had previously obtained permission from the County Council but had not had the necessary number of buses ready to run an efficient service, now took over the Halifax to Rochdale route on a 90-minute frequency. In the meantime Halifax Corporation had received the last 6 of its new Karrier CL6s, 5 of which were placed in service in December 1927 (31/3-6 : CP6221/3-6) with 32 (CP6222) following in January 1928.

On 1 May 1928 a Ministry of Transport enquiry took place into the use of bus stands in the centre of Halifax following numerous complaints by local shop owners. At this time there were nine different bus operators (including the Corporation) running services to places outside the town and in addition there were the Corporation Borough routes which collectively caused a deal of congestion in the town centre. King Edward Street and Wards End were used for Corporation services while Southgate, used by many of Hebble's routes, was not desirable in the public interest. There were also objections to the possible use of Alexandra Street and thus some form of regulation appeared to be essential. Before the situation could be resolved, however, on 6 June the Town Council approved an agreement with O. & C. Holdsworth for the running of its Hebble buses between Hebden Bridge and Halifax on a joint basis. This resulted on 27 June in the granting of licences to Holdsworths between Halifax and Blackshaw Head and Widdop Gate with a fare of 6d each way between Halifax and Hebden Bridge in order to relieve the former chaos. Meanwhile, since Halifax Corporation had now withdrawn its service between Midgley and Mytholmroyd, permission was given by Midgley District Council to F.Sutcliffe of Cragg Vale to operate from Midgley through to Hebden Bridge. At this same time the Railway Road Transport Bill was going through Parliament, giving the railway companies powers outside London to provide and operate motor omnibuses throughout the country, subject to a protection given to municipal transport undertakings in respect of tramways, trolley vehicles and motor omnibus services within the boundaries of their areas. However, Halifax Town Council was of the opinion that the protection offered was inadequate and that this should be extended to the motorbus services which such undertakings were now providing outside their boundaries.

Somewhat surprisingly, in the late spring of 1928 Halifax Corporation purchased a new Karrier Z-type chassis which it fitted with a body built in its own workshops at Skircoat Road. Numbered 49 (CP6692) and equipped with a polished wood table, oak panelling, and 14 individual armchair-type seats, it was intended mainly for use as a Committee bus but in the event it saw little use after it was first licensed on 6 June 1928 and was withdrawn on 8 January 1930 and offered for sale. During August and September a further 6 new Karrier buses (43-8 : CP6925-30)

were placed in service by the Corporation for normal passenger use, these being of the 3-axle WL6 type which featured improved braking, were powered by 6-cylinder Dorman 6.59 litre petrol engines, and were fitted with dual-door 32-seat bodywork by Harris & Hassall.

Following a conference held on 29 September at Brighouse Municipal Offices between representatives of Bradford, Huddersfield, Halifax and Brighouse Councils to discuss the running of buses between Halifax and Brighouse via Hove Edge and Slead Syke and also from Halifax to Bailiffe Bridge via Hipperholme and Lightcliffe, Halifax Corporation began to operate both routes on 1 October despite the necessary consents still needing to be obtained and extended the Brighouse service to Rastrick. The Halifax to Brighouse section was already covered by the Calder Bus Company and thus the two operators were now in competition with one another. With little option but to look to the future, the Tramways and Electricity Committee met on 2 October to discuss a report explaining the running powers which had now been conferred on the railway companies by their Road Transport Acts of that year and a meeting between the Corporation and the railways companies was arranged with a view to arriving at an agreement which would afford protection to the Corporation's tram and bus services within the Borough. On the following day it was decided that the terminus of the Sowerby motorbus service should in future be at the Star Inn and not Steep Lane whilst at the same meeting of the Town Council amendments were made to the regulations relating to the stands and stopping places of buses in the town, specifying that on stands occupied by authorised buses they may stop for longer than is necessary for the purpose of picking up and setting down passengers provided that this time did not exceed ten minutes. It was also agreed to revise the stands for the following services :

Heptonstall, Widdop Gate, Burnley, Midgley, Copley, Beech Road - north side of Westgate.
Siddal-King Cross - south side of Wards End
King Cross-Siddal - north side of Wards End
Old Station-Warley - east side of Church Street
Circular via Parkinson Lane - east side of Southgate
Circular via Hanson Lane/Norton Tower - west side of Southgate
Wainstalls/Illingworth/Brighouse via Hove Edge - west side of Cow Green
Bradshaw - west side of Carrier Street

As had been expected, the LMS Railway Company was not long in applying for licences and on 3 October Sowerby District Council granted the licences to enable the Company to maintain a service of buses between Halifax and Rochdale via Blackstone Edge and between Halifax and Rishworth as well as granting Hebble Bus Services licences for a service from Halifax to Manchester via Sowerby Bridge and Rochdale. Soon afterwards on 9 November, the Tramways Committee in Halifax was instituted to take responsibility for all tram and bus affairs, thus replacing the previous Tramways and Electricity Committee.

The first bus to run in the north of England by the LMS under its recently acquired powers did so on 10 December 1928 over the Halifax to Rochdale via Blackstone Edge moorland route, a distance of 18 miles. 12 trips were made in each direction, augmented at weekends, and the service operated to the railway stations at both Halifax and Rochdale to enable passengers by rail to easily connect with the buses. The vehicles employed on this new operation were powerful Leyland Lions with bodywork built by the Railway Company in its own workshops at Derby and the inauguration of this service resulted in the cessation of Rochdale Corporation's operations over the same route. The LMS lost no time in applying for licences to Midgley, Luddenden Foot and Hebden Bridge Councils for services between Halifax and Midgley and Halifax and Hebden Bridge and Heptonstall and it was agreed that a joint advisory committee of eight local authorities should be set up to deal with motorbus control or licencing of vehicles to which the LMS application was referred. This committee was known as the Joint Advisory Committee for Calder and Ryburn Valleys.

In the middle of December 1928 all the local councils were asked by West Riding County Council for observations on the Halifax Corporation Bill asking for powers to run motor omnibus services through their districts without the necessity of applying for the consent of the respective councils. Greetland District Council, in particular, expressed disquiet as it felt it was suffering an injustice through the Halifax action in fixing fares and refusing

Squeezed between other buses in King Edward Street, Halifax, 34 (CP6224), a Hall Lewis-bodied 3-axle Karrier CL6 picks up its passengers whilst working the Rishworth via Ripponden service Behind it is 39 (CP5123), a Hall Lewis-bodied Karrier CL4 acquired with the business of Ryburn Garage & Transport Co. Ltd. in November 1927. *R.Marshall*

to allow private operators vehicles to pick up passengers between Halifax and West Vale. Indeed, it felt that it was impertinent for Halifax to ask for facilities which it was not prepared to grant to others.

1929 began, and on its second day Halifax Town Council granted the LMS licences for 12 vehicles to ply for hire on the following routes :
(1) Halifax - Luddenden Foot - Midgley.
(2) Halifax - Mytholmroyd - Hebden Bridge - Heptonstall.
(3) Halifax - King Cross - Beech Road.
(4) Halifax - Brighouse - Lower Edge.

On the following day Hebble took over the services of the Calder Bus Company in the Brighouse, Hipperholme and Bradford areas. These had been previously been sold to Bradford Corporation who, before physically taking them over, found that it did not, in fact, have any operating powers outside the city boundary. A week later on 9 January, the Halifax Corporation Bill was presented to a meeting of ratepayers in the Borough, this seeking powers to run buses on any of its tram routes outside the town boundary and also on eight specified services for which the consent of the County Council had not been obtained. Additionally, it contained a section stating that if the Corporation wished to run motorbuses other than those mentioned, it might do so with the consent of the local and road authority and Ministry of Transport which should not be unreasonably withheld. By a large majority the Bill was approved by the meeting. On 16 January Walton & Helliwell was granted a licence by Mytholmroyd District

Council to ply for hire with the motorbus previously owned by J.A.Halliday between Cragg Vale and Mytholmroyd while on 6 February Halifax Watch Committee granted licences to the LMS Railway Company to run from Halifax to Bradford via Shelf and also via Queensbury, to Keighley via Denholme and Bingley via Denholme. Also on this day the Joint Advisory Committee of the Calder and Ryburn Valleys advised its member authorities not to oppose the Halifax Corporation Bill despite there still being resistance from Hebden Bridge District Council. By 20 February the LMS had taken over the Halifax to Lower Edge, Rastrick via Brighouse service from Halifax Corporation, thus confirming its continued growth.

On 13 March the Halifax Corporation Bill was approved by a Select Committee of the House of Lords, helped by an agreement which had been reached between the Corporation and West Riding County Council prior to it coming before the Parliamentary Committee. The powers of the Corporation to run buses was, however, restricted to the routes which extended a distance no greater than 14 miles from Halifax Town Hall whilst one of the 8 specified services (Draper Lane - Heptonstall - Slack Bottom - Blake Dean) was deleted as it was deemed not to be suitable for buses. The Corporation was also advised to introduce workmen's fares on its buses as well as trams. The provisions of this Bill and the formation of the Joint Committee a few weeks later were to set the pattern of bus services in Halifax and its surrounding districts for the next 40 years, thus removing a state of disorder in local bus services which had existed since 1924.

Alphabetical List of Despatches.

Add the name of the County when addressing your letters.

	a.m	a.m	a.m	p.m	p.m	p.m	p.m	p.m	p.m	p.m
Skipton	6 15	9 45	1045	1230	..	..	..	..	..	1030
Southport	9 15	1045	..	4 30	7 15	..	9 45	..	..	1030
Southowram	6 0	..	..	..	..	..	..	..	..	..
Sowerby Bridge..	5 0	6 0	1030	2 0	..	..	..	..	..	1030
Stockport	6 15	9 15	1045	1 0	4 30	..	9 45	..	..	..
Todmorden	9 45	1 0	..	..	..	..	..	..	..	..
Triangle	5 15	..	4 30	12 0	..	..	..	..	..	1030
Wakefield	6 15	9 45	1045	1230	..	5 0	..	..	..	1030
Wales	6 15	1045	..	4 30	7 15	8 0	9 45	..	1030
Wigan	6 15	1045	..	4 30	7 15	8 0	9 45	..	1030
Wolverhampton..	6 15	1230	3 45	4 30	..	5 0	9 45	..	..
York	9 45	..	..	..	4 30	7 30	9 0	..	..

Attention is drawn to the exceptions shewn
in the List of Outward Mails.

§ Saturdays only   * Saturdays excepted   ‡ Wednesdays only   Parcels
⁴ Wednesdays excepted

General Night Mail 8 p.m., secures 1st delivery most places in England.

MOTOR BUS LETTER BOXES

All leave p.m.	Mon. to Fri.	Saturday	Sunday
Barkisland			
Bradshaw	8·30		
Brighouse	7·42	7·30	
(via B'ugte.)	8·30	7·42	5·30
Brighouse v Sth	8·23	8·30	6·42
Causeway Foot	7·30, 8·10		7·0
Claremount,		8·23	
Boothtown	7·5	7·18	5·23
Hebden Bridge	6·43, 7·33, 8·13		6·50
	8·33		
Heptonstall	7·58	6·43, 7·33	
Hullen Edge	8·37		5·33
Illingworth	8·8	8·8	
(via Mix.)	6·55		
Midgley		6·55	
Mill Bank	7·0, 7·30		
Norland(M'c'k)	7·25	7·30	
Northowram	7·30		6·50
Pellon	7·25, 8·55,	8·0	
Queensbury	7·50, 8·50	7·25.	
Rishworth	7·13, 8·13		5·55
Shibden	6·25, 8·45		6·50
Siddal	6·40	7·20	6·13
Skircoat Green	7·17, (7·27 Fri. only) 7·12		6·5
(Cir. Bus to West End)			6·17
Southowram	8·0		6·23
(via Pinnar L.)			
Sowerby (S.L.)	6·45	8·0	
Stainland (O'lo)	7·12, 8·55		5·30
Wheatley		6·45	
Wainstalls	7·20	7·10	
Craggvale from	6·47		6·12
Hebden Bridge	6·5		6·40
Heptonstall	6·25	5·55	6·32
from Hebden Bridge		6·25	

13

SETTING UP THE JOINT OMNIBUS COMMITTEE

Shortly after receiving their road powers, the Railway Companies approached Halifax Corporation with regard to the joint working of motor omnibus services and representatives of the Corporation attended meetings at the LMS offices at Hunts Bank, Manchester in September 1928 to discuss the possibility of co-ordinated working on a much closer basis than was formerly known, namely by interested financial co-ordination as well as timetable co-ordination. During the intervening months several more meetings took place to consider the many and varied points of view and to define the clauses of the joint working agreement. The negotiations concerning this agreement with the Railway Companies were not only lengthy, but of an intricate nature involving numerous financial problems although the final result was judged to be in the mutual interest of Halifax Corporation, the LMS and LNE Railway Companies and, not least, the travelling public, not only of Halifax but also the surrounding districts particularly by eliminating wasteful competition. Owing to the proposals for the joint working agreement with the Railway Companies, the consent of the parties affected were obtained to the clauses in the 1929 Halifax Corporation Bill which would have undoubtedly been severely opposed under other conditions. The arrangements were concluded in time to be brought into operation on 1 April 1929 whereby the Railway Companies became associated with the Corporation in the operation of some existing omnibus routes which travelled outside the Borough, namely :

(a) Halifax - Huddersfield.
(b) Halifax - Bailiff Bridge.
(c) Halifax - Sowerby.
(d) Elland - Sowerby Bridge.
(e) Halifax - Brighouse - Lower Edge, Rastrick.
(f) Halifax - Hebden Bridge - Heptonstall.
(g) Halifax - Luddenden Foot - Midgley.
(h) Halifax - Beech Road, Sowerby Bridge.

These were to be controlled by the Joint Omnibus Committee consisting of four representatives of the Corporation and four nominees of the Railway Companies. The arrangements provided that any omnibus service which may be developed further afield to and from Halifax would be operated by the Railway Companies and the first meeting of the Joint Omnibus Committee was held at the Kings Cross Hotel in London on 18 April 1929 under the Chairmanship of Arthur Gledhill of Halifax Corporation. The Chairman was to alternate in successive years between the Corporation and nominees of the Railway Companies and the venue of the meetings was to similarly alternate between Halifax Town Hall and places nominated by the Railway Companies. It was agreed at the first meeting to extend the Ryburn Valley, Sowerby, Beech Road, Midgley and Heptonstall services in Halifax to terminate at the Old Railway Station to provide connections with the railway and to this end buses left the station approach 4 minutes earlier than the advertised departure times then proceeded to their respective stands in the town centre.

The opening fleet of the Joint Omnibus Committee comprised 28 buses (3 Dennis 50-cwts and 25 Karriers), all of which were transferred from the Corporation. 14 of them continued to be owned by the Corporation while the other 14 were purchased by the Railway Companies to fulfil their part of the agreement although all were placed under the direct control of the Joint Omnibus Committee as a separate entity. The fleet livery was the same as that of the Corporation and thus there was no necessity to instigate a repainting programme. The process of consolidation began immediately and on 31 March 1929 the Brighouse - Bailiff Bridge tramway service passed into oblivion with JOC buses taking over the following morning to mark the very first day of Joint Committee trading.

Negotiations which had begun the previous November between the LMS and LNE Railway Companies and Hebble Bus Services for the purchase of the latter were finally completed on 2 May 1929. It was pointed out that arrangements had been made with Halifax Corporation regarding certain motorbus routes and the purchase of the Hebble business was suggested as Halifax was a convenient operating centre for both Lancashire and Yorkshire services which could be extended in either direction, an argument which Hebble eventually acceded to. Under the agreement which was dated back to 1 January 1929, the Railway Companies took over all the Hebble services, equipment and its premises at Walnut Street, Halifax. The Commercial Street site which had been purchased by Hebble a few years earlier was leased to the Railway Companies for twelve months and O. & C. Holdsworth were to undertake the supervision on behalf of the Railways. Since inaugurating their services in December 1924 with 8 buses, O. & C. Holdsworth's fleet had grown to 86 - mainly Albions - which were employed on 28 routes. The Railway Companies immediately announced their intention of commencing several new services including Halifax to Manchester, Wakefield, Bradford via Holmfield and Bradshaw, Scarborough and Sheffield with the Railway Stations being the terminal points and its booking offices additionally being responsible for the new bus services. The tendency appeared to be that as the bus services developed, the railway services to smaller stations would be curtailed, although business would carry on as normal as far as the public was concerned with, in the fullness of time, additional facilities being provided for the comfort and convenience of passengers.

At the second meeting of the Joint Omnibus Committee on 7 June 1929 the request by Brighouse Council for JOC buses to operate along Halifax Road from Hove Edge to Brighouse was acceded to whilst the service between Halifax and Bailiff Bridge was to be discontinued from 4 December. Following meetings on 10 and 11 June, it was confirmed that the routes operated by Hebble Bus Services from Halifax to :

(a) Elland & Huddersfield.
(b) Barkisland.
(c) Beech Road & Midgley.
(d) Southowram & Brighouse.
(e) Hullen Edge.
(f) Heptonstall.

were to be transferred to the Joint Omnibus Committee for its sole operation. To provide the additional vehicles needed to implement this change it was agreed to transfer 13 Hebble buses to the Joint Omnibus Committee fleet, 9 of which were required to maintain these services and 4 as spares. Although the deal was struck on 1 April 1929 when the JOC agreed to purchase part of the Hebble undertaking for £36,000 which included 'Consideration' as a going concern for five years and the net value of the buses taken over, it was not until 1 November 1929 that the purchase was actually completed and five days later that the transfer of the portion of the Hebble undertaking actually took place. As a consequence, 2 Leyland SG9s, 9 Albions of various types and 2 Karriers were then transferred from Hebble to the JOC in whose fleet they were given numbers 70-82, none of which survived for more than a few years, however, with the last being withdrawn and sold in 1934. Prior to this, the Corporation had taken delivery of its last new bus of Karrier manufacture in the form of a Hall Lewis-bodied 32-seat rear entrance JKL (50 : CP8006) which took up its duties in June. This was the first of three buses which had been ordered for evaluation purposes, the other two - Leyland TS2 52 (CP8008) and dual door English Electric-bodied Dennis EV 51 (CP8007) - joining the fleet in November 1929 and February 1930 respectively.

The arrangements for the operation of services under the November Joint Working Agreement were as follows :

(1) All omnibus services solely within the Borough boundaries were to be operated by and on behalf of the Corporation. These routes were designated 'A' services.

(2) The Corporation was to operate services which extended beyond the Borough boundary within a prescribed area (red area) on behalf of the Joint Omnibus Committee. These routes were designated 'B' services.

(3) Long distance services, beyond the territory of the above two areas, were to be operated entirely by the Railway Companies or their nominees. These routes were designated 'C' services.

(4) Protection was to be given to the Halifax Corporation tramways both inside and outside the Borough.

(5) Passenger motor omnibuses were to be provided to meet the needs of the services adequately, as to one-half by the Railway Companies and one-half by the Corporation.

(6) The omnibus fleet was to be managed and maintained by the Joint Omnibus Committee, and the receipts (after deduction of the operating expenses) were to be paid one-half to the Railway Companies and one-half to the Corporation. Any deficit arising from the working was to be borne by the parties in a like manner.

(7) The joint services were to be operated by the Tramways and Omnibus Department of the Corporation under the direction of the Joint Omnibus Committee, and were to be arranged so as to secure co-ordination of working with the railway system.

(8) The companies were to pay the Joint Omnibus Committee a percentage of all fares received from passengers picked up and set down by their 'C' services within the area controlled by the Joint Omnibus Committee.

(9) Financial arrangements :

   (a) The capital invested in the fleet of omnibuses was to be provided as to 50% by Halifax Corporation and 50% by the Railway Companies.

   (b) The receipts less operating expenses were to be divided in the same proportions.

   (c) The Corporation half was to be brought into account against the charge for interest on capital and depreciation of omnibuses, the latter being charged for at the rate of 20% on the original cost, so that the cost of omnibuses would be met in five years.

   (d) The Railway Companies were to charge their own depreciation against the balance of receipts, but interest on capital was to be replaced by dividend on shares.

   (e) All other charges were to be apportioned as follows :

     (*I*) Garage accommodation - An agreed rent to be charged for the use of Corporation premises and proportioned to Tramways, 'A' services and 'B' services.

     (*ii*) General Management expenses - These were likewise to be proportioned on an agreed basis : Tramways, 'A' services and 'B' services.

     (*iii*) Garage repairs and maintenance - These were to be carried out in the Corporation workshops and garages and the actual cost was to be debited to the Joint Omnibus Committee.

     (*iv*) Petrol - to be supplied by meter and charged to the joint account.

     (*v*) Drivers and conductors wages - these were to be paid weekly by the Corporation and reimbursed monthly from the banking account.

     (*vi*) Banking account - a separate banking account was to be kept in the name of the Joint Omnibus Committee and operated by cheques signed by the Chairman and accounting officer.

Thus, in financial terms, all the services maintained solely within the Borough were classed as 'A' services and the revenue from these passed to the Corporation. All revenue from the JOC or 'B' services running over routes that *did not* penetrate the Borough went to the JOC. However, the revenue from the JOC services which *did* enter the Borough was multiplied by the fraction 33.262 divided by 184.961 and 21% of the result was passed to the Corporation to represent inside Borough passenger fares taken on JOC vehicles. Additionally, every Hebble bus running into the JOC area that stretched from Heptonstall to Brighouse had to list separately the value of tickets sold within that area and 25% of the total passed to Halifax coffers to be split in the ratio of 1 part to the 'A' services and 4 parts to the JOC 'B' accounts. Also, the Yorkshire Woollen District Transport Co. made a compounded payment to the JOC as well as handing over to the Corporation 25% of all fares taken on its buses within the Borough and similarly Huddersfield JOC also made a payment to the Corporation for the same basic reason. Complicated this certainly was, but it worked!

On 6 July 1929 the first railway line closure to passenger traffic took place since the LMS had been granted road powers, this being the Sowerby Bridge - Ripponden - Rishworth branch whose traffic was then transferred to the bus services. A month later on 8 August, an off-shoot of the King Cross service was started with buses diverting at the junction of Haugh Shaw Road and Savile Park Road and then operating via Bell Hall, Savile Park, Birdcage Lane and Scar Bottom to Washer Lane. At this same time Stainland District Council granted licences to the JOC to operate along Broad Carr Lane to Station Road at its junction with Stainland Road and also granted licences for the Halifax to Stainland (Black Horse Inn) service on the understanding that the Corporation would introduce competitive fares. The latter service commenced on 1 September with 2 buses as a result of which the West Vale - Stainland branch became the third railway line to close for passenger traffic since the LMS had gained its road powers. The buses acquired for this new operation were a pair of Leyland PLSC3 Lions (83/4 : CH7903/9) which were transferred from the LMS and had bodywork built by the Railway Company at its Derby works.

November 1929 marked yet another milestone in the history of road passenger transport in Halifax when the Corporation received its first ever double deck buses. Numbering 3, these were of the new AEC Regent type and were fitted with 50-seat Short Bros bodies which featured an open rear staircase and

Displaying Inner Circle via Parkinson Lane in its front destination aperture and carrying oval-shaped posters in its upper and lower deck side windows to publicise the new circular service, Short Bros-bodied AEC Regent 54 (CP8010) awaits its passengers in Southgate in 1929. Its open staircase and humped roof were a familiar feature of all the double deckers purchased by Halifax between 1929 and 1933.
R.Marshall collection

New in February 1929 and exhibited at the Commercial Motor Show at Olympia, London in Glasgow Corporation's orange, green & cream livery, Short Bros-bodied AEC Regent demonstrator MT2114 was purchased by Halifax Corporation in February 1930 and numbered 57. So impressed with its livery were its new owners that they adopted this as their new standard colours.
R.Marshall collection

humped roof to allow a centre upper deck gangway. Given fleet numbers 53-5 (CP8009-11), a further bus of this combination - 56 (CP8167) - joined its sisters on the Inner Circle route in January 1930. Powered by 6-cylinder petrol engines of 6.1 litres capacity, the double deckers soon proved their capability on the hills of Halifax and, obviously delighted with its new buses, the Corporation immediately placed an order with AEC for a further 4 for use in the Joint Omnibus Committee fleet. In the meantime arrangements were made for the purchase of another bus of this combination which had previously been used as a demonstrator by its manufacturer and was the prototype of this new model. New in February 1929 and registered MT2114, it was initially demonstrated to a number of operators around the country before being repainted into Glasgow Corporation's orange, green and cream livery in preparation for its display at the Commercial Motor Show at Olympia, London in November of that year. Purchased by the Corporation immediately after the Show ended, it eventually arrived at its new home early in 1930 and was quickly placed in service on 17 February still adorned in its Glasgow colours. So impressed was the Tramways Committee with this livery that it was decided to adopt it as Halifax's new standard and a repainting programme was quickly put in hand to thus transform the fleet.

Seeking further expansion, on 20 December 1929 the Joint Omnibus Committee completed its negotiations with G.Garrad & Sons of Greetland to take over its operations and vehicles of which the Corporation received a half share. Garrad's fleet comprised 4 Albions, a Gilford and a pair of 16-seat Gotfredson buses, all of which were placed in the JOC fleet with effect from 1 January 1930 although the Gotfredsons were not used by their

new owner and were transferred to the Corporation for use as goods vehicles later in the year. Complaints were soon received about the services taken over, particularly from Greetland and Stainland Councils, that the timetable was not being adhered to and the buses used were in a deplorable condition. Indeed, so many had broken down that passengers had no confidence in riding up hill. It was said in reply that most of the vehicles taken over had been in poor condition and that there had been little opportunity to put them in a proper state of repair. As a result of these complaints, however, it was decided to return 6 buses (1 Karrier and 5 Albions) to their makers for complete overhaul and to recondition their bodywork in the Tramways workshops at Skircoat Road. In order to cover their temporary withdrawal, 4 new Albion PM28 buses (CH7927/8/32/7) were hired from the LMS Railway Company and 1 new Albion PM28 (UP1370) from the LNE Railway Company from 1 February.

Early in January 1930 the Ministry of Transport gave its consent to the JOC for two services from Greetland (Wall Nook) to Barkisland School, one running via Rochdale Road, the other via Turbury Lane and Butterworth Lane End whilst at this same time the Brighouse service from Halifax was revised to also operate to Lower Edge via Bonegate as well as Slead Syke. Later, on 5 February it was decided that on completion of the road improvements in Rochdale Road and Darcy Hey Lane the King Cross bus would proceed to Washer Lane and return via the Moor while the Woodhouse Lane bus would go forward to King Cross and come back via the Trafalgar Inn with a 3d fare for the complete journey. Meanwhile, a 2d universal fare was applied to the Inner Circle route, this proving successful both in terms of increased revenue and passenger numbers. On 19 March the

Tramways Committee took the decision to operate the Warley service via Barum Top and Hopwood Lane instead of by way of West Parade and Park Road as well as to run for a trial period of three months a circular service to Siddal via Wards End, New Road, Water Lane, Jubilee Road, Salterhebble Hill, Huddersfield Road, Shaw Hill and New Road at a universal fare of 2d. Buses from King Cross to Siddal were to operate via Horton Street, Old Station and Church Street instead of New Road with passengers being allowed to continue to the Old Station at no extra charge while on 16 April the service from Warley to the Old Station was discontinued and buses were to proceed from Wards End via Skircoat Road and Skircoat Green to Copley Village. In May 1930 the Joint Omnibus Committee urged the Calder and Ryburn Joint Bus Services Committee to take legal action in all cases where unlicenced bus services were operating since the JOC services in local districts were not paying their way.

At the beginning of July 1930, the first two of the four AEC Regent double deck buses (66-9 : CP8168/646-8) ordered for the JOC fleet were placed in service on the Halifax - Huddersfield route upon which they were joined by the other two when they were delivered in September. Although completely satisfied with its new buses, upon learning of a new diesel engine which was being fitted to the AEC Regent chassis, the Tramways Committee at its meeting on 19 November agreed to purchase a bus of this type for comparative trials against its petrol-engined double deckers. The price of the diesel-engined AEC Regent was £2,018

which was slightly higher than that of its petrol-engined counterpart, although specifically favourable terms were negotiated for this test vehicle which, it was understood, would reduce running costs in the region of 2d per mile. Equipped with a Short Bros. body of similar design to those already in service in Halifax, it had an AEC A155-type 8.8 litre engine which, being around 4 inches longer than the equivalent petrol engine necessitated the fitting of a longer bonnet and the radiator being moved forward by a similar amount. Numbered 58 (CP9061), it entered service on 27 March 1931.

Prior to this date, the Town Council took the monumental decision on 7 January to replace its trams with motor buses on parts of five routes : Triangle to Sowerby Bridge; Shelf to Stump Cross; Queensbury to Boothtown; Brighouse to Stump Cross and Southowram to New Bank. The Savile Park/Warley Road and Skircoat Green routes were to be left in abeyance until after an experiment with buses which were to run from town via Savile Park to King Cross and thence Warley Road to Parkinson Lane top where they would connect with the West End/Pellon trams.

This rearward view of the upper deck of English Electric-bodied AEC Regent 119 clearly shows its humped roof which allowed additional headroom along the centre gangway. *K.A.Jenkinson collection*

A lower deck view towards the rear of English Electric-bodied AEC Regent 119 when new in 1932 provides a glimpse of its open staircase. *K.A.Jenkinson collection*

This would do away with the Outer Circle route and buses from West End would proceed down Parkinson Lane and Stanley Road to return to King Cross and Halifax via Savile Park. For the replacement of trams on the above services an order was placed with AEC for a further 10 Regent double deckers and in addition it was agreed to purchase from Martin Chalmers the Elmwood Estate situated at Shaw Hill containing 10,600 square yards for the erection of a motorbus depot for the sum of £3,000. Prior to the start of the tramway replacement programme, Halifax had, with the exception of Glasgow and Manchester, a greater tram mileage outside the Borough than any other town in Britain.

On 12 February the JOC reported that the Railway Companies had made a payment of £500 in respect of passengers being picked up and set down in the red area by the 'C' services whilst at the same time it was decided to take action to protect the JOC's operational interests under the provisions of the Road Traffic Act 1930 in making an assessment of the effects of the competition by taking a check on every motorbus service which competed with those of the JOC. At the following meeting a formal objection was made to every application for a road service licence which in any way affected the JOC services in the red area, the objection being particularly related to the imposition of protective fares. Special waybills and tickets were to be used on all 'C' routes, including J.Hirst of Ripponden who had now become Ripponden & District Motors, for all passengers both picked up and set down in the red area from 20 April 1931.

At its meeting on 4 March 1931 the Town Council approved the purchase of 4 additional AEC Regent double deckers and also 4 AEC Regal single deckers for Corporation use as replacements for the last of the 50-cwt Dennis single deckers which were now six years old and were becoming costly to maintain and whilst Hoyal bodywork was specified for the Regents, English Electric

Typifying Halifax's early fleet of AEC Regents, Corporation English Electric-bodied 119 (CP9445) illustrates the open rear staircase and humped roof which was a feature of all these buses.

were again given the contract for the single deckers. Soon afterwards in April, the Joint Omnibus Committee took delivery of 3 of its English Electric-bodied AEC Regals (91-3 : CP9064-6) with the fourth (94 : CP9067) following in May and in July these were joined by 7 Hoyal-bodied AEC Regent double deckers (85-9/95/6 : CP9062/3/79-81/68/9) of which a further 9 (107-15 : CP9070-8) were delivered to the Corporation fleet in July, largely for tram replacement purposes.

Standing in the doorways of Skircoat Road depot ready for their next day's service are four of the undertaking's humped-roofed AEC Regents. *K.A.Jenkinson collection*

Joint Omnibus Committee 101 (JX44), an AEC Regal fitted with an English Electric body which incorporated a Scottish-style rear entrance is seen prior to its entry into service in 1932. *D.Akrigg collection*

The first official tram abandonment, however, had already taken place on 6 May when the last trams ran between Hove Edge and Brighouse. Replaced the following day by four buses (1 single and 3 double deckers) on the Bonegate and Stead Syke routes, this provided a 15 minute service between Thornton Square, Brighouse and Halifax with the through running to Lower Edge being discontinued. Extra buses were to be run between Brighouse and Hove Edge to connect with the trams until reduced fares were sanctioned between Brighouse and Halifax. The tramway terminus was to be Hipperholme during the day and Hove Edge in the morning and evening peak hours.

The Traffic Commissioners, under the Road Traffic Act 1930, were now assuming responsibility for all types of public road transport licensing and all the applications for licences by the Joint Omnibus Committee and Corporation were contained in the no.3 issue of Notices and Proceedings dated 24 April 1931 including new services between Elland and Norland and Elland and Outlane. On 3 June the Town Council took a decision that was to play an important part in municipal transport in Halifax, this allowing the use of Crossfields as a bus park suitable for through traffic and standing places for buses during 'cooling' and lay-over time.

The first sitting of the Yorkshire Area Traffic Commissioners to deal with applications for licences by the JOC and Corporation took place at Huddersfield on 12 July. Yorkshire (Woollen District) Electric Tramways objected to the continuation of the Corporation's Halifax - Bradshaw service because of the difference in fares (the Corporation charging 3d against Y(WD)ET's 6d on its Halifax - Keighley service between Halifax and Ovenden) and additionally objected to the Halifax - Huddersfield Joint service because of the workmen's fares between Elland and Halifax. The Corporation lodged objection to E.J.Slater & Son of Elland continuing its Rastrick (Sun Inn) - Halifax and Elland (Lower Edge) - Halifax services on the grounds that there were already more than sufficient buses plying between Elland and Halifax and that the hilly routes were not safe nor suitable for motorbus operation. Also, the Corporation felt that it should not have to co-ordinate with services which had been running unlicensed in Halifax over a number of years despite refusals, appeals and prosecutions. However, an appeal to the Traffic Commissioner resulted in E.J.Slater being granted permission for his services to operate through Elland to Halifax (King Edward Street) and later, on 16 June 1932, the Joint Omnibus Committee announced arrangements for the co-ordination of both services and also between J.W.Halstead's and the JOC's services between West Vale and Halifax.

The next stage of the tram replacement programme was implemented on 22 July 1931 with the withdrawal of trams on the Southowram route and their substitution by buses and a week

later on 29 July a similar arrangement was applied to the Halifax - West End via Savile Park route. The replacement buses on the latter charged a 2d universal single fare although a 2d return fare was made available between West End and St.Judes Church, Savile Park. With its purchase of Elmwood Park completed, the Town Council on 5 August authorised the Tramways Committee to erect a new omnibus depot on the site in accordance with the plan submitted by the Borough Engineer, the cost of which was estimated at £25,000.

Following the introduction on 23 September of a trial bus service between Commercial Street and St.Luke's Hospital, Dudwell Lane upon which a 2d single fare was charged, a deputation from Southowram District Council met with the Tramways Committee to discuss the extension of the Southowram route to Towngate on the grounds of the dangers in reversing at the Pack Horse Inn. After giving this some consideration it was agreed by the Committee on 16 December and implemented soon afterwards. Shortly before the year ended, the Corporation received 3 (121-3 : CP9447-9) of its 4 English Electric-bodied AEC Regal single deckers while the JOC gained 2 identical buses (97/8 : CP9440/1), these being the first buses in the fleet to be equipped with Clayton Dewandre saloon heaters..

During the first two months of 1932 both the Corporation and JOC fleets were enhanced by the arrival of a number of new AEC Regents, the 5 for the Corporation (116-20 : CP9442-6) having English Electric double deck bodies and the solitary example for the JOC (90 : CP9439) being fitted with a Hoyal body while the Corporation in February also received its outstanding AEC Regal single decker (124 : CP9450).

At the Joint Omnibus Committee on 11 February, a letter from the Ministry of Transport stating the arrangements in respect of the issue of licences to Railway and Municipal Joint Committees was read, its content being as follows :
(I) Public Service Vehicle licences would be issued in the name of that one of the constituent bodies of the Joint Committee to which each vehicle belonged.
(ii) Road Service licences would be issued in the name of all constituent bodies of the Joint Committee jointly.
The allocation of the Joint fleet, to comply with this legal requirement was allocated as follows :

One of a pair of English Electric-bodied AEC Ranger single deckers bought by the Joint Omnibus Committee in 1932, 132 (JX50) was, together with its sister, withdrawn from service shortly before the war ended and was sold in May 1945 to a Leeds dealer. *R.Marshall collection*

(a) Vehicles attributed to Halifax Corporation ownership - 25 (8 Karrier, 2 Dennis, 6 Albion, 1 Leyland and 8 AEC)

(b) Vehicles attributed to LNER ownership - 6 (2 Karrier, 2 Albion and 2 AEC)

(c) Vehicles attributed to LMS ownership - 19 (5 Karrier, 1 Dennis, 4 Albion, 1 Leyland and 8 AEC)

At the following Joint Committee meeting which was held on 15 April an arrangement with Hebble Motor Services was ratified in that 35% of gross receipts of all passengers picked up and set down in the portion of the red area specified below was to be paid over to the JOC on all the following services :

Halifax - Shelf - Bradford and Halifax - Shelf - Leeds : between Halifax terminus and Bottomley's Arms, Shelf.

Halifax - Queensbury - Bradford : between Halifax terminus and Queensbury (Cenotaph).

Halifax - Bingley : between Halifax terminus and the County Bridge, Denholme Clough.

Halifax - Wyke : between Halifax terminus and White Horse Inn, Whitehall Road, Hipperholme.

Hipperholme - Bradford : between Brown Horse Inn, Hipperholme-Denholme Gate Road and Bottomley's Arms, Shelf.

Halifax - Burnley and Halifax - Edge Hey Green : between Halifax terminus and Slack Bottom, Heptonstall.

Halifax - Rochdale ; between Halifax terminus and White Hart Inn, Ripponden.

The fares and stages were to be co-ordinated with those of the JOC within the area concerned and separate tickets provided by the JOC were to be issued for these journeys.

As the summer drew to a close, more new buses arrived for the JOC fleet in the form of 4 AEC Regal single deckers (99-102 : JX42-5) and 3 AEC Regent double deckers (103-5 : JX46-8) all of which carried English Electric bodywork and were placed in service in August and 2 AEC Rangers with 20-seat English Electric bodies (131/2 : JX49/50) which were first licensed in September for use on lightly trafficked routes. These were joined in October by the first coach to be operated in the Joint Omnibus Committee fleet, this being a 32-seat Burlingham-bodied AEC Regal 4 which dated from 1931 (125 : WX7668) and was purchased from C.Avison of Huddersfield. Meanwhile the Tramways Committee on 5 August decided that owing to the poor condition of the tram track between Stump Cross and Northowram a bus service should be introduced between Halifax and Northowram (Borough boundary) but that the trams should continue operating between Northowram and Shelf with the service being co-ordinated with the existing 'C' services on the Halifax - Shelf section. To this end the tram service between Halifax and Northowram ceased on 16 August with the replacement buses taking over on the following day. This, however, did not meet with universal favour due to the inconvenience caused by the change of vehicles at the Queen Victoria Inn, Northowram, but nevertheless the Corporation continued to run the trams in order to retain a right to maintain a

One of five English Electric-bodied AEC Regals purchased in 1933 for the Joint Omnibus Committee fleet, 127 (JX327) prepares to leave its King Edward Street terminus on a journey to Mill Bank in August 1948, six months before its withdrawal from service.   *R.Marshall*

service to Shelf!

The new Elmwood bus garage, after a lunch at the White Swan Hotel in Halifax, was officially opened on 4 November 1932 by the Mayor of Hailfax, Alderman Rufus Stirk OBE, JP. who declared that it was quite a decent garage which would prove worthy of the outlay on it. Problems had been solved for the engineer in the design of the buildings to house the new type of vehicle for servicing, cleaning, washing and inspection between each daily run to give the most constant and efficient service on the road. It was in close proximity to the tramshed, Skircoat Road bus garage and workshops as well as Halifax town centre, thus reducing dead mileage. There were only four columns in the whole floor area and it was built with lattice girders 14ft 6in and 120ft span, the roof having 300 tons of steel. There was no wood apart from the doors and the main entrance was wide enough to allow four vehicles abreast with proper power operated fuel pumps and adequate washing facilities with pits for greasing and examination. A turntable was provided in the centre to facilitate parking of buses and there were four large extractor fans discharging direct to the outside through ducts. Everything considered, it was a masterpiece! However, there was a delay in bringing the new garage into operation since a high tension boiler was only delivered a day before the official opening and the roof of the heating chamber had to be left open to get the boiler in position and connected. The necessary work on this section's reinforced concrete roof and the lagging of the boiler with asbestos material was responsible for the delay and it was not

This view inside Elmwood depot early in 1932 shows 65 (a Gilford acquired with the business of G.Garrad), AEC Regents 57 (MT2114) and 68 (CP8647) and AEC Regal 94 (CP9067), all except 57 being Joint Omnibus Committee vehicles. *K.A.Jenkinson collection*

The side-mounted engine of Halifax Corporation's solitary AEC Q-type double decker no.7 (JX1461) seems to be creating a deal of interest to the two gentlemen standing alongside it when it was delivered in March 1934. *T.Worsnop collection*

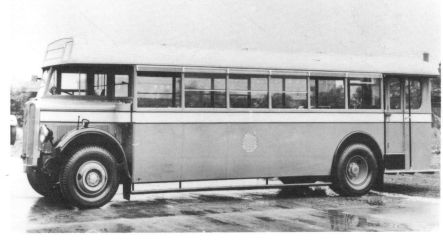

Unusually fitted with a Scottish-style rear entrance body by Park Royal, AEC Regal 143 (JX1954) was one of two such buses purchased new by the Joint Omnibus Committee in 1934. *R.Marshall collection*

until 29 November that the Corporation and JOC fleets of buses (which had risen from 28 to 90 in the space of five years) were able to use the new depot.

On 21 December it was agreed that the Halifax - Pellon tram route, which incorporated Spring Hall Lane and Warley Road, should be abandoned and a bus service introduced which would link up with the Outer Circle (Savile Park - West End route) at some future date at a universal fare of 3d in each direction. In addition it was decided to allow Hebble Motor Services Ltd (which had been sold to a new company early in 1932 in which the Railway Companies still retained a half share) to operate over the route from Northowram to Shelf as it seemed that there would be unnecessary duplication which was not warranted by traffic and the service could be satisfactorily handled by the Hebble services between Halifax, Leeds and Bradford. The abandonment of the Stump Cross to Shelf tramway thus took place on 31 March 1933.

Having found its diesel-engined AEC Regent purchased in 1931 to have been a reliable and cost effective vehicle, the Corporation during the following year placed an order for a further five buses of this type fitted with English Electric double deck bodywork. Making their debut in January 1933, 2-6 (JX321-5) surprisingly still featured an open rear staircase and thus had a somewhat dated appearance at a time when most other operators had abandoned this styling. Fitted with 8.8 litre engines they were, however, well suited to tackle the numerous hills around Halifax and proved popular with drivers and passengers alike. Later, in May the Joint Omnibus Committee also took delivery of the first 3 of a batch of 4 buses of this same combination (133/5/6

: JX331/3/4) together with 3 English Electric-bodied AEC Regal single deckers (126-8 : JX326-8) of which a further 2 (129/30 : JX329/30) arrived during the following month. The remaining AEC Regent (134 : JX332), however, did not appear until the final month of the year for some inexplicable reason.

On 31 March, the Caddy Field service was discontinued as a result of its disappointing loadings and it generating less than 5d per mile in revenue terms while towards the end of the summer on 16 August a new service was started between Halifax and the Merry Boys Inn at Shibden at the request of residents in Brow Lane and Shibden Valley. Continuing the tramway abandonment programme, electric traction ceased between Stump Cross and Hove Edge on 30 September.

The death of the Tramways General Manager Walter Theodore Young from pneumonia on 5 April at the early age of 53 came as a severe shock to all those associated with the Corporation and Joint Omnibus Committee and necessitated the advertising for a replacement at an early date. From the various applicants George Frederick Craven, who was a director of Park Royal Coachworks, London and had earlier been manager of Reading Corporation Transport, was selected on 26 September. Prior to him taking up his new duties at Halifax on 1 November, the Town Council at its meeting on 25 October decided that the present type of letter posting box should be affixed with attachments in an easily accessible position to the public together with driver observation to all Corporation motorbuses at a cost of £50 in total and at the same time it was agreed to apply for licences to enable the Corporation to operate motorbuses in case of breakdowns on the tramways at tram fares and also in connection with late night trains, dances and social events etc. from specific points of the tram routes - e.g. Alexander Hall, Marlborough Hall and from any part of the Corporation area (tramways and local bus routes). This application became extremely protracted, however, and the appropriate licences were not granted until August 1934.

In the meantime, on 14 December 1933 the JOC set up a sub-committee to commence negotiations for the purchase of the local service of Ripponden & District Motors and those of E.J.Slater & Son and J.W.Halstead. It was also recommended that the JOC services between Elland and Outlane and Halifax and Outlane via Stainland should remain as existing until midday after which the Elland - Outlane service was to proceed via Park Lane, Forest Hill Road and Gosport Bridge to Outlane and return via the main road to Stainland with the Halifax - Outlane route operating this circuit in the opposite direction.

On 20 December, the worst and most spectacular accident involving a Corporation or JOC bus occurred when AEC Regent no.2 (JX321) working the 9.0pm Northowram to Halifax journey

Amongst the vehicles taken over from Ripponden & District Motor Services in September 1934 was Taylor-bodied AEC Reliance WX2073 which was given fleet number 149 by its new owner, Halifax Joint Omnibus Committee in whose livery it is seen here soon after its acquisition.
R.Marshall collection

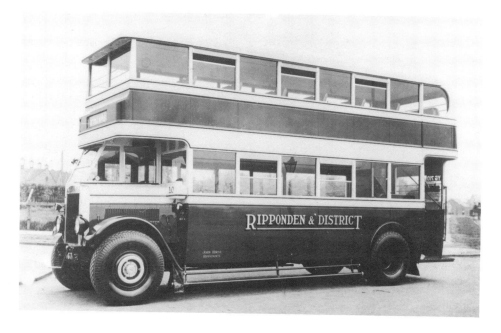

Seen when new in 1932 is Ripponden & District Motor Services all-Leyland lowbridge-bodied TD2 10 (YG710). Taken over by Halifax Joint Omnibus Committee in September 1934 and numbered 148, it was sold in July 1936 to Western SMT at Kilmarnock. *R.Marshall collection*

Displaying the original style of Joint Committee logo on its side panels which was lettered 'Halifax Corporation & Railway Services', all-Leyland TS2 151 (WX3260) was one of the five buses acquired from Ripponden & District Motor Services in September 1934. Despite being repainted into its new owner's colours, it gave little more than a year's service and was withdrawn and sold towards the end of 1935.
R.Marshall collection

skidded on the icy road at Upper Brear, Stump Cross and then careered over a wall and down an embankment towards some houses below. It was reported 'that one could only marvel that this mammoth six and a half ton vehicle had not continued its fall and demolished the houses below. Apparently a slight ledge had arrested its progress after overturning'. Four passengers on the bus were injured whilst the bus was badly damaged and punctured by stones. It was recovered by dragging it up the embankment by means of two tram rails and helped by two heavy lifting cranes and turned back onto its wheels on reaching the road. Following a vast amount of repair and rebuilding work the bus was returned to service during the spring of 1934.

As the year drew to a close the Council decided that the tram service to Stump Cross and that between King Cross and Gibbet Street Barracks should be discontinued from 9 January 1934, although in the event the latter was deferred until a new circular bus service could be licensed between Halifax and West End in conjunction with the St.Luke's service which was to run via Fountain Street, Bull Green, King Cross Lane, King Cross, Warley Road, Barracks Corner, Gibbet Street, Westholme Road, Hopwood Lane, Bull Green and Rawson Street to Commercial Street in both directions. This was designed to relieve congestion on the Savile Park and West End services as well as on the Inner Circle route. Meanwhile the tram service to Stump Cross was to be curtailed to Shibden park but to operate only at the evening peak and on Saturdays and Sundays with increased services on the Northowram bus route.

Following a breakdown in talks between the JOC and E.J.Slater & Son of Elland, the latter sold its bus operations to the Yorkshire (Woollen District) Electric Tramways Company who was then granted licences to operate on the Halifax to Lower Edge and Halifax to Rastrick services against which the JOC lodged an appeal. During the following month the tram service between King Cross and West End finally ceased on 4 February with its replacement circular bus service commencing on the next day. Due to a vehicle shortage caused by this, an additional bus was obtained by the Corporation on hire from AEC at Southall initially for a six month period. An AEC Regent with Park Royal body, it was registered MV3522 and dating from 1932 had been previously used by its manufacturer as a demonstrator.

On 16 February agreement was finally reached between the JOC and Ripponden & District Motors for the purchase of the latter's bus services between Halifax and Rishworth, Halifax and Mill Bank and Ripponden and Sowerby Bridge via Mill Bank together with 5 buses for the sum of £12,000 and an option was given for the JOC to purchase Ripponden & District's Elland to Ripponden service together with 1 bus at some future date. The

buses involved in the deal comprised 1 AEC Reliance and 2 Leyland Tiger single deckers and 2 Leyland TD2 double deckers fitted with Leyland lowbridge bodywork which featured a sunken gangway in its upper deck. In the event, however, it was not until 7 August that the takeover actually took place despite the Rishworth service being revised ahead of this date on 25 July and similarly the Halifax - Mill Bank service on 1 August.

In the meantime, Halifax Corporation placed a revolutionary new type of double deck bus in service on 1 March 1934 in the form of an AEC Q-type which had its petrol engine mounted at the offside of its chassis, thus allowing the passenger entrance door to be located at the extreme front opposite the driver. Numbered 7 (JX1461), Its English Electric body incorporated seating for 59 passengers but due to its lack of a door to its front entrance, it proved cold and draughty in winter and caused discomfort to its lower deck passengers and conductor alike. With its engine prone to overheating and its lack of road adhesion particularly on wet roads with stone setts, it never proved to be a popular bus and spent most of its short working life on the Southowram and Savile Park - West End routes.

On 1 April the tram service from Halifax to Queensbury was curtailed to run only as far as Boothtown and a new bus service was introduced by the JOC to cover the whole route from the town centre to the Ring O'Bells at Queensbury which was a steep climb for most of the way. A month later on 15 May the decision was made to also abandon the tramway between Sowerby Bridge and Triangle whilst the extension of the Sowerby Bridge to Hubberton bus service commenced on 23 May. Prior to the latter events, on 17 April the West Vale service of J.W.Halstead of Greetland was taken over by the JOC together with a 20-seat Commer Centurion which was given fleet number 106 by its new owner and remained in service until 1936.

Early in May 4 new AEC Regent double deckers were placed in service, 10/1 (JX1788/90) in the Corporation fleet and 137/8 (JX1787/9) in that of the Joint Omnibus Committee and not surprisingly in view of the Tramways General Manager's previous employment, these were fitted with Park Royal bodywork which incorporated an enclosed staircase. Also in May, the Corporation hired a further AEC Regent from its manufacturer on a long term basis to assist it with its tramway replacement programme. Registered AMV482 and fitted with a Park Royal enclosed staircase body it had previously been used by AEC as a demonstrator. In July the JOC received a further 2 new Roe-bodied Regents (141/2 : JX1914/5) as also did the Corporation (12/3 : JX1912/3). To increase the size of their fleets and provide sufficient buses to enable the tramway abandonment programme to forge ahead, the Corporation and the JOC collectively received 10 more new buses between August and December with the former taking 2 English Electric-bodied AEC Regent double deckers (14/5 : JX2037/8) and the JOC 2 identical buses (139/40 : JX2039/40), 4 AEC Regents with Chas.Roberts bodywork (152-5 : JX2297-300) and 2 AEC Regal single deckers bodied by English Electric (145/6 : JX2106/7). Together these replaced the last of the Karrier single deckers in each fleet, the Corporation's solitary Dennis EV and the last of the JOC's Albion PM28s and Leyland PLSC3s.

During the course of delivery of the above new vehicles, on 6 August 1934 buses replaced trams on the Halifax - Boothtown service whilst in September permission was given to the JOC to run services to the Royal Oak, Lower Edge and the Sun Inn, Rastrick from Halifax via Elland. Although in the event neither were operated by the JOC and the application was subsequently withdrawn, this move was sufficient to force an amended operating agreement with Yorkshire (Woollen District) Electric Traction Company under which the latter was to pay 25% of its receipts from passengers picked up and set down entirely in the Corporation and JOC areas and the JOC was to cease operating the Brighouse - Lower Edge route and support Y(WD)ET in its application for this service and the Elland - Rastrick routes which were to become through routes from Brighouse. At this same time, 27 September, arrangements were made for the Corporation to receive from the JOC 25% of revenue for all passengers picked up and set down between the following points on JOC routes :
Halifax - Outlane, Greetland, Barkisland, Hullen Edge, Norland (Halifax - Salterhebble).
Halifax - Brighouse via Southowram (Halifax - Southowram).
Halifax - Brighouse via Hipperholme (Halifax - Stump Cross).

Making its way along Commercial Street, Halifax in 1948, a few weeks before being withdrawn from service is JOC English Electric-bodied AEC Regent 139 (JX2039) which dated from 1934. *R.Marshall collection*

Halifax - Queensbury (Halifax - Boothtown).
Halifax - Huddersfield including Huddersfield JOC (Halifax - Salterhebble).

This came into force on 7 November 1934 on the cessation of the tramway between Salterhebble and Stainland following revisions to the bus services on the routes affected which required 4 additional double deckers. Application was also made to the Traffic Commissioner by the Corporation for the running of an excursion to the recently-opened reservoir at Gorple via Slack Bottom, Heptonstall which actually commenced the following Easter.

On 19 December agreement was reached for the hire of another AEC Regent from its maker, on this occasion for evaluational purposes in view of it being fitted with a Park Royal body of a new all-metal construction. Given fleet number 24 and registered CML516 it had previously been used as a demonstrator and entered service in the Corporation fleet in January 1935 at the same time as 5 new AEC Regents with Chas.Roberts bodywork. 3 more of the latter combination made their debut in service in February by which time, as a result in the increase in size of the bus fleet, the Corporation and JOC were now using the old motor omnibus depot and part of the tram depot at Skircoat Road in addition to the Elmwood garage for their buses.

Meanwhile, the tramway abandonment programme continued with the closure of the Salterhebble route on 31 March when a revised arrangement was made with the JOC. Rather than extend the General Hospital (St.Luke's) and Siddal services to Jubilee Road, Salterhebble the Corporation allowed the JOC to pay 25% of the receipts (with revised fares) on the following portions of routes in the Borough, not all of which were affected by the Salterhebble tram service closure, commencing on 1 April and thus replacing the previous agreement :

Halifax - Outlane, Barkisland, Norland, Hullen Edge (Halifax - Greetland Station).
Halifax - Huddersfield (Halifax - Calder & Hebble Inn, Salterhebble).
Halifax - Brighouse via Southowram (Halifax - Cock & Bottle Inn, Southowram).
Halifax - Brighouse via Hipperholme (Halifax - Mytholm).
Halifax - Queensbury (Halifax - Stocks Gate).
Halifax - Sowerby, Rishworth, Ripponden, Beech Road (Halifax - Rochdale Road, Borough boundary).

The Corporation, however, continued to run with buses a peak-hours only service to Salterhebble to cater for traffic requirements.

In April 1935 as a result of a petition from residents, a new bus service was started on an experimental basis between Halifax (Westgate) and Boothtown running via Southgate, Russell Street, Northgate, New Bank and Claremount Road and following its

Proudly displaying Regal and Oil-engined badges on its AEC radiator, Corporation Roe-bodied 29 (JX3424) is seen here prior to its entry into service in 1935.
R.Marshall collection

successful operation it was made permanent on 19 June. In the meantime at the end of May the Siddal and Washer Lane (circular) routes were linked together while on 1 June the Cragg Vale service of Walton & Helliwell of Mytholmroyd was taken over by the Joint Omnibus Committee together with a 20-seat Commer Centaur and a 31-seat Leyland LSC1 Lion. Due to its age, the latter was not, however, operated by its new owner and was instead quickly sold. At the beginning of August at a meeting between the JOC and Sowerby Bridge District Council, a new circular bus service was proposed for a two-month trial period between Wharf Street, Bolton Brow, Park Road, Beech Road, Tuel Lane, Burnley Road, Albert Road, Gratrix Lane and Bolton Brow which would link up with another circular route round the Beechwood Estate in Sowerby. It was also decided to extend the Elland - Sowerby Bridge service to Triangle to relieve the heavy volume of passenger traffic as well as conduct a survey to see if a morning service was required to Mill Bank and in addition licences were applied for to vary the frequency of the Halifax - Steep Lane, Hubberton services with journeys alternating between the two and additional peak workings between the Royal Hotel, Sowerby Bridge and Hubberton/Steep Lane.

Perhaps realising its mistake in specifying open staircase bodywork for all its new double deckers delivered up to December 1933, it was decided in mid-September 1935 to experimentally enclose the staircase of one of its older AEC Regents at a cost of

£70 and after completing this conversion, agreement was reached that other buses of this type should be similarly treated. In the event, however, it was only those delivered new in 1933 to the Corporation and JOC that were rebuilt in this manner and during the process these had their capacity increased from 50 to 53 by the fitting of three additional seats to their upper decks. A few days later on 2 October, the Tramways Committee Chairman stated that the 2 AEC Regents hired in May 1934 were being paid for out of revenue by means of a mileage charge and when this equalled the cost of the buses they would then become Corporation property. It would appear, however, from vehicle taxation records that this had already been achieved and that the 2 buses concerned had already passed to Corporation ownership some eight months earlier!

The final new buses to be taken into stock during 1935 made their debut in November and December and on these occasions were all AEC Regal single deckers of which the Corporation received 6 (3 with Roe bodywork and 3 with Park Royal bodies) and the JOC 2 (1 each with Roe and Park Royal bodies). Numbered 25-30 (JX3420-5) and 157/8 (JX3426/7) respectively, these replaced the Corporation's Leyland TS3 and the JOC's AEC Reliance and 2 Leyland TS2s to leave both fleets standardised on AEC products except for 2 Leyland TD2s and 2 Commers.

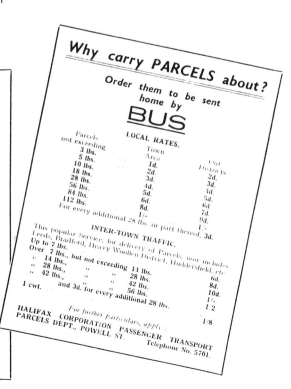

REACHING THE END OF THE LINE

As 1935 drew to a close, the decision was made to abandon the tramway between Tuel Lane and Hebden Bridge as soon as sufficient buses were available for the replacement service. This was planned to take place on 31 March 1936 under an arrangement that for six years following the changeover the JOC was to pay the Corporation one half of the additional net receipts accruing from the Halifax - Midgley, Halifax - Heptonstall, Cragg Vale - Hebden Bridge and the proposed Halifax - Hebden Bridge service using the year ending 31 March 1936 as the base year. This effectively meant that the Corporation was to receive 9d out of every 1/- profit made while passengers would have the increased benefit of time saving, apparent from the fact that the buses were already carrying three quarters of the traffic on the route.

At the meeting of the Town Council held on 5 February 1936 an idea to provide two bus stations - one at Crossfield, the other at a proposed site in Market Street and Union Street - was floated. As most of the latter site was fronted by houses and business premises and as it was estimated that at the peak hour of operation 81 buses would be entering and leaving the proposed bus station by means of Market Street, this was felt to be unsatisfactory in terms of increased congestion on a busy thoroughfare.

were used initially as tramway replacement vehicles on the Hebden Bridge route although they also allowed the withdrawal of the Commer Centurion and the 2 ex.Ripponden & District Leyland TD2s which coincidentally were the last double deckers in the fleet of lowbridge configuration.

On 22 July the Tramways Committee decided that the Wheatley service should be diverted to run via City Lane and Hebble Lane while on 5 August the Town Council passed a resolution for the Borough Engineer to prepare plans and estimates for a bus station and car park at Crossfield, Halifax. The objective was that if only a portion of buses used it, this would relieve some of the congestion in the town's streets upon which there were bus stands. It was stated that there was no reason why a second bus station should not also be built as soon as a suitable site was found and that in the meantime around 25% of the buses running into the town would find Crossfield the best site.

On 5 September the Elland to Ripponden service of Ripponden & District Motors was taken over by the JOC, but on this occasion no vehicles were involved in the deal, while on 8 October the JOC decided to discontinue the through tickets which had been available between Halifax and Todmorden by tram and bus.

As part of the celebrations following the winning of the cup by Halifax Rugby League Football Club, JOC English Electric-bodied AEC Regal 92 (CP9065) was decorated with bunting and used to convey the team around the town.
R.Marshall collection

About to leave its stop outside Woolworths in King Edward Street, Halifax on a journey to Norland on the 56 service is JOC 1937 Park Royal-bodied AEC Regent 174 (JX5267). *R.Marshall collection*

The new circular service between Tuel Lane and the Beechwood Estate commenced on 27 January 1936 whilst the extension of the Elland - Sowerby Bridge route to Triangle and the service of workmen's buses to Mill Bank began on 2 March as did the improved services to Hubberton and Steep Lane. Since 23 March, the services of F.A.Sutcliffe (Vale Bus Service), Mytholmroyd had been operated on hire by the JOC between Cragg Vale and Hebden Bridge pending the receipt of licences to give an even service with that taken over from Walton & Helliwell during the previous year. This was also to be co-ordinated with the Halifax - Hebden Bridge service between Mytholmroyd and Hebden Bridge from 1 April when the tram service was replaced by buses. Included with the F.A.Sutcliffe business which was purchased by the JOC for £700 was a 20-seat Bedford WLG bus, although this was not used by the JOC and was quickly sold.

Although no new buses were purchased by the Corporation fleet during 1936, the JOC benefited with the arrival of a further Park Royal-bodied AEC Regal single decker (159 : JX3428) in January and 12 new Park Royal-bodied AEC Regent double deckers (160-71) in March and April. Of the latter, numbers 169 and 171 broke new ground by being the first buses in either fleet to be fitted with fluid flywheels and pre-selector gearboxes. Most

Passing along Market Street, Halifax close to the end of its journey from Southowram on route 30 is Corporation Park Royal-bodied AEC Regent 45 (JX6429) which was new in April 1938.   *D.Akrigg collection*

Taking a rest in Alexandra Street, Halifax in 1948 before departing to Copley is Corporation Park Royal-bodied AEC Regal 52 (JX6559) which was new in 1938.
T.Worsnop collection

Although 1937 began quietly, at a meeting of the Town Council on 3 February it was resolved that having provided a parking place which may be used by PSVs on the Crossfield site situated between St.James Road, Gt.Albion Street, Orange Street and Broad Street with the exception of 2,202 sq.yards on the east side, that it should make an order appointing that parking place as a station for PSVs to the Ministry of Transport for confirmation. A car park had to be made before the Town Council could make a bus station, but the car park would then be used only by PSVs despite still officially classed as a car park. No vehicle standing on that park could ply for hire at that time but if the order was made, the vehicles which the Town Council allowed to stand there could then ply for hire. Confused? Well who wouldn't be! There was, however, a wave of dissent to this, since the Corporation, under the 1929 agreement with the Railway Companies, had a duty to co-ordinate as far as possible its services with trains from the railway station.

In February it was decided to purchase for £725 the AEC Regent bus which had been on loan to the Corporation since the previous year while between April and June 4 new Park Royal-bodied AEC Regents (31-4 : JX5261-4) were added to the fleet together with 8 identical buses for the Joint Omnibus Committee (172-9 : JX5265-72). These further increased the size of both fleets as the only withdrawals during 1937 were one of the JOC's 1930 vintage AEC Regents and its solitary Commer Centaur. At the start of October, however, the Corporation hired a number of buses to Huddersfield Joint Omnibus Committee for a few weeks for use on its Birkby route which it was converting from tram to trolleybus operation. Unfortunately owing to road lowering at one point on this service, the Huddersfield undertaking was not able to start running its trolleybuses immediately and thus had to substitute motor buses until this work was completed.

From 9 November 1937 the name of the Halifax's Tramways Committee was changed to the Passenger Transport Committee since the tramway operation was now the smaller part of the undertaking which comprised 40 trams and 130 motorbuses of which 95 were double deckers (59 diesel and 36 petrol engined) and 35 were single deckers (18 diesel and 17 petrol engined). Prior to this, route numbers had been allocated to all the Corporation and JOC services for the first time.

The saga of the new Crossfield bus station was still far from settled and on 18 November an enquiry was held at Halifax Town Hall in respect of the proposal. Usage of buses in streets waiting at their respective stands was causing a great deal of concern to the Highways Committee as there were 21 Corporation, 22 JOC and 19 other operators routes (including express services) which used the centre of town for departures and in the teatime peak hour 163 buses left from the central area. Crossfield bus station had first been used for the August Wakes Saturday departure for tours and excursions by 107 coaches. The location of the bus station was opposed by the LNE and LMS Railway Companies, other motorbus operators, Halifax Corporation Market Tenants Association and other businesses with the Railways Companies complaining that it would set back co-ordination between road and rail. It was alleged that it was inappropriate for all services to use Crossfield, although its use had been recommended initially for only 5 routes despite the fact that it had manoeuvrable spaces for 29 vehicles on a gradient of 1 in 16.5. The commercial

New to the Joint Omnibus Committee in 1939, AEC Regal 193 (JX6581) was fitted with a handsome looking Roe body of rear entrance configuration. Seen in Market Street, Halifax before the outbreak of World War II, it was waiting to take up its next duty on service 50 to Brighouse.
R.Marshall collection

element complained that the site was ill chosen and would change the location of shop traffic whilst other bus operators were not keen to have their services, particularly to and from the north-east direction, diverted away from the town centre. And so the arguments continued ....

By the end of 1937 the tramway had been reduced to 23 miles of track compared with 60 miles in 1929 while during that same period the bus route mileage had increased from 57 to 170. No sooner did 1938 start than the tramway shrunk yet further with the cutting back of the Causeway Foot service to Mason Green on 18 January and the introduction of a replacement bus service on the following day. A month later on 16 February, the decision was taken to similarly abandon the Halifax - West End via Pellon Lane and Spring Hall Lane tram route with effect from 31 March and to operate in its place two circular bus routes, one of which was to run in both directions to Pellon New Road, Sandbeds Road to the top of Albert Road, thence down Albert Road and Spring Hall Lane before returning to town, the other operating from Arcade Royale via Skircoat Road, Heath Road, Free School Lane, Savile Park, King Cross, West End, Barracks Corner, Spring Hall Lane and Pellon Lane to the town centre in both directions. This was, in fact, a continuation of the existing West End via Savile Park service and was to be co-ordinated with five other routes in the area. As a means of providing these additional services 12 new Park Royal-bodied AEC Regents entered service with the Corporation between March and May (35-46) with a further 3 arriving in June (47-9) together with 4 Roe-bodied AEC Regal single deckers (50-2/7). Simultaneous with these, the Joint Omnibus Committee placed in service in June an AEC Regal with

Park Royal bodywork (188) together with 6 Regals (189-94) and 8 Regents ((180-7) which were all bodied by Chas.H.Roe.

On 3 August 1938 the fate of the tramway was sealed when the Town Council took the decision to abandon the remaining routes in favour of motorbuses at the earliest convenient time and to this end it placed its largest order ever for new buses which called for no fewer than 34 double deckers. Although there was a combined net profit of £32,000 for the year ended 31 March 1938, the tramway was still making a loss, albeit smaller than in previous years as a result of the reduced track mileage. The abandonment resolution was carried unanimously and progress was quickly made when, on 24 August, the Highroad Well service was converted from tram to bus operation due largely to the need for urgent track repairs on some sections of this route. This had been the first of two routes, with King Cross, in the system, opening on 29 June 1898 from Commercial Street to Highroad Well via Gibbet Street. The discontinuance of trams on the Halifax - Tuel Lane and Halifax - Sowerby Bridge routes took place on 29 November and the replacement service on the following day was undertaken on the same basis as that for the tramway between Tuel Lane and Hebden Bridge with half of the additional receipts accruing on the four existing and one additional JOC services being paid to the Corporation for a period of six years. The Corporation was also to operate a bus service from the Old Station via the town centre, King Cross, Burnley Road, Cote Hill, Bairstow Lane, Willow Hall Lane, Rochdale Road and King Cross back to town in both directions using four buses.

The first 16 of the new buses, AEC Regents with Roe bodywork (59-65/8/72-9), made their service debut during

November and December and in addition to being used for tramway replacement purposes, they also allowed the withdrawal of 6 of the Corporation's older petrol-engined Regents, 4 Regals and its solitary AEC Q-type which was last used in June 1938. Additionally the Joint Omnibus Committee took 6 petrol-engined Regents and 7 Regals out of service during the year following the arrival of its new buses in June.

Following the receipt by the Corporation of 18 more new AEC Regents (53-6/8/66/7/9/70/1/80-7) in January and February 1939 of which 6 had bodywork by Chas.H.Roe, 8 by Park Royal and 4 by Weymann, the trams ran their final journeys on the remaining route to Mason Green, Ovenden on St.Valentines Day 14 February 1939 and thus, after 41 years, Halifax's tramway operations finally came to an end. At the dinner to commemorate the occasion, Alderman A.H.Gledhill, Chairman of the Passenger Transport Committee, said 'that the success of the new buses

was so pronounced that the Council had ordered them in ever increasing numbers since 1929 until nine years later the undertaking had 130 double deckers and 35 single deckers with a further 42 buses on order. The buses were negotiating the steepest gradients in the British Isles and they had almost completely changed over from petrol engines to heavy oil compression ignition engines, such was the rapidity of progress in innovation, which gave nearly double the mileage per gallon without fire risks (145 buses were now of this new type). From that night a uniform system of fares would be in operation throughout the whole of its traffic area with all other bus operators, with the exception of the Manchester to Bradford express service which was not for local traffic'. An improvement was made the following day to the Causeway Foot service as well as the commencement of the Beechwood Road route.

In April 1939 the Joint Omnibus Committee also received 4 new AEC Regent double deckers (200-3) fitted with Park Royal metal-framed bodies, although one of these (200 : JX6939) was not to remain long in its original mechanical state and was within a few days of its entry into service fitted experimentally with a centrifugal clutch as a couple of months earlier had Corporation Regent 63 (JX6896). Later, on 18 May the General Manager Mr.Craven demonstrated to experts at a meeting of the Yorkshire and Lancashire Municipal Transport Association a Corporation

Seen in typical Halifax surroundings, Joint Omnibus Committee Park Royal-bodied AEC Regent 203 (JX6938) climbs past the Commercial Hotel a few weeks before the outbreak of World War II
T.Worsnop collection

AEC Regent (64 : JX6897) fitted with a supercharged forced induction engine which he had invented. The Rootes-type supercharger was belt driven from the transmission between the fluid flywheel and gearbox and its main features were a 33.3% increase in horsepower that eliminated black smoke and gave a saving in fuel costs with 6.5 miles to the gallon. It could be fitted for £100 and enabled gradients of 1 in 9 to be climbed at 26 mph with quick recovery of speed after restarting on hills. Claimed to be the most powerful bus in Britain, 64 was tested on the Northowram and Queensbury routes, taking the steep hills with ease, reducing noise and providing a steadier balance. Soon afterwards the 4 AEC Regents delivered to the JOC in April were similarly converted.

Although at a meeting of the Council it was agreed to make some alterations to the services in the Ovenden area, these were subject to the events which were unfolding in Europe at that time and following the declaration of war in September these had to be

temporarily deferred. Meanwhile, in July the Joint Omnibus Committee added 5 new Roe-bodied AEC Regents (204-8 : JX7706-10) to its fleet and in August took delivery of 2 Park Royal--bodied AEC Regal single deckers (196/7 : JX7702/3). These, together with the 4 Regents taken into stock in April, enabled 5 Regents and 4 Regals - all petrol engined examples - to be removed from service along with 7 of the Corporation's petrol-engined Regents, but rather than being sold the Regals were placed in store for possible re-use should the hostilities escalate. Of the Corporation Regents, 2 (107/14 : CP9070/7) were loaned to Coventry Corporation from January 1939 and were ultimately sold to that undertaking in April 1940 without returning to their native Halifax. The last new buses to be received during 1939 were an AEC Regal (195 : JX7701) and 2 Leyland Cubs (198/9 : JX7704/5), all three of which were fitted with Park Royal bodywork and entered service in the JOC fleet in September.

The last new double deckers to be placed in service by the Joint Omnibus Committee before the outbreak of World War II were Roe-bodied AEC Regents fitted with 8.8 litre engines. One of these, 204 (JX7706) is seen in Halifax town centre working the 44A service to Hubberton.   *J.Fozard*

HELPING HANDS

Associated with the course of events prior to the outbreak of World War II on 3 September 1939 was the sale to the Corporation for £35 each of the JOCs two AEC Ranger single deckers (131/2 : JX49/50) for Air Raid Precaution Ambulance purposes, these being followed soon afterwards by four AEC Regals (99-102 : JX42-5) for similar purposes. Another bus sold in connection with the war effort was Corporation AEC Regent 119 (CP9445) which was disposed of to the Headquarters of Northern Command at York. Soon after the hostilities commenced, it was agreed by the Council that the Civil Defence Ambulance Service should be housed at the Passenger Transport depot and thus the scene was set......

The first effects of the war were quickly felt when, on 23 September, reduced services were implemented on several routes due largely to the rationing of motor spirit, the first casualties being the rural services to Heptonstall, Cragg Vale, Illingworth via Mixenden, Copley, Queensbury, Elland - Barkisland, Bradshaw, Rishworth, Causeway Foot and Stainland with the Elland to Norland route being withdrawn completely. Many of the above services were either curtailed or reduced in frequency with the last departures from the town centre being altered to around 9.00pm. Additionally, the windows of all the Corporation and JOC buses were painted dark blue to block the light emanating from them during the hours of darkness and in the blackout periods.

From the beginning of January 1940 a special service was operated between Huddersfield and Brighouse and Acre Mills at Old Town, Hebden Bridge for the transport of Cape Asbestos Company workers with two journeys in each direction each day whilst by 3 February some relaxation enabled buses to once again run through to Mount Tabor and Copley although the Queensbury service continued to operate only as far as Catherine Slack. Other routes to be reinstated were that between Elland and Barkisland and the Bradshaw route as far as Bradshaw Lane, with the Rishworth and Stainland routes being reinstated along their complete length. Additional running time was now being allowed, particularly on JOC services, as a result of the introduction of reduced lighting allowed on buses. During the following month the last new vehicle to enter service until after the end of the war did so on 6 March in the form of an AEC Regent (88 : JX8106) fitted with an all-metal Park Royal body which was added to the Corporation fleet. Soon after this had taken up its duties, experiments began in May in the use of creosote oil as an alternative fuel and as a result of the headway made by Halifax in this direction certain evening services were able to be extended to 10.45pm. Twelve buses were converted to run on a mixture of crude oil and creosote with the supercharged examples using a 50/50 mixture and the non-supercharged buses running on a 30% creosote, 70% crude oil combination as there were no restrictions on either of these fuels as there were on petrol.

Meetings of the Joint Omnibus Committee now had a number of new venues including the Kings Cross Hotel, London; Royal Victoria Hotel, Sheffield; Crewe Arms Hotel, Crewe; Grand Hotel, Leicester; Midland Hotel, Manchester and the Midland Hotel, Derby, the changes being due in most cases to the exigencies of the war situation. Amongst the items discussed at these meetings were the precautions to be taken by staff in the event of enemy air attacks and to this end instructions were given to all drivers that when sirens sounded they were to use their own discretion to continue operating. If these was actual danger, drivers were to pull to one side of the road, turn off all the vehicle's lights, see that passengers had opportunity for leaving for shelter and then take shelter themselves. It was also decided that the JOC should be placed on the priority supply lists for certain firms

manufacturing PSVs so that as little delay as possible in delivery would be experienced in purchasing new vehicles scheduled for 1940/41.

In August it was decided to extend the Washer Lane - Jubilee Road service to the Backhold Lane Estate, Siddal, permission for this being granted on 2 October as well as for the operation of double deckers on the other of the Siddal routes (Wards End - Bailey Hall Road - Swan Bank Lane) to the existing terminus at Jubilee Road to avoid duplication by single deck vehicles. It was also decided that from 7 October all evening services would be curtailed between 9.15pm and 10.0pm. Revisions to the Mixenden, Illingworth, Ovenden Way, Nursery Lane and Bank Top services, as previously arranged, came into operation on 27 November 1940 while having not so long ago pronounced against the employment of women as conductors, the Council decided to reverse this decision as a result of the long hours being worked by traffic employees and the number who had been called up to serve in the armed forces.

A great deal of interest was caused in London by the appearance of Halifax buses on the streets of the capital after an appeal by the Regional Traffic Commissioners was made on 21 October 1940 to provincial transport undertakings. Halifax responded with alacrity sending 8 AEC Regents (4 each from the Corporation and JOC fleets) and its contribution was the first to arrive reaching London two days later, to the astonishment of the London officials. Two of the buses entered service the same day (Park Royal-bodied 10/11 : JX1788/90) being allocated to Riverside (Hammersmith) garage for use on service 11 (Shepherds Bush - Liverpool Street) while two others ran on this same service from Dalston garage from the following day. The remaining four were all allocated to Forest Gate garage for services 25B (Aldgate - Becontree Heath) and 25C (Forest Gate - Victoria) and of the eight 142 (JX1915) wore a grey livery and 171 (JX3737) grey with light brown bands - both experimentally introduced since the start of the war - while the remaining six were in Halifax's standard hue. 'The Halifax bus' according to the Times correspondent, 'was a handsome one, dressed in orange and green with narrower bands of cream, the Borough coat-of-arms on the orange panel on each side, and much like the capital's most modern buses in size and shape'. During their stay in London they also operated from Tottenham and Hanwell garages before all returning to Halifax in July 1941, each bearing

One of several buses loaned to London Transport by Halifax from October 1940 to July 1941, Corporation Park Royal-bodied AEC Regent 11 (JX1790) with masked headlights and white painted wing tips makes its way through the capital's centre on a journey to Shepherds Bush on route 11.
R.Marshall collection

a metal plaque 'London 1940-1941' as a token of that service. Prior to the arrival of these buses in the capital, however, on 10 October the JOC had loaned its two Leyland Cubs (198/9 : JX7704/5) together with AEC Regent 140 (JX2040) to the LNE Railway Company's London District. The Regent which was used by the LNER to transport military personnel from Wembley to Stanmore was returned to Halifax early in January 1941 whilst the Leyland Cubs remained in London throughout the war and were eventually returned to their native Halifax on 14 April 1946. A further bus loaned to another undertaking for a short period was JOC AEC Regent 104 (JX47) which was sent to assist Sheffield Corporation on 18 December and returned home on 4 January 1941.

With no signs of an end to the war being in sight, the restrictions on services and vehicle and street lighting etc. continued whilst concern was expressed for women conductors being out on the streets at any time up to midnight after a few had been accosted. A proposal to provide buses before and after normal service to take female employees to and from their homes was agreed at a meeting on 3 December 1941, although there was some dissent since they were doing a man's job and as such should be treated the same. In view of this, the facility was extended to all employees but was to be reviewed after November 1942. In the meantime from the middle of November 1941 the existing bus service between Washer Lane and Park Lane, Siddal was, with the exception of the hours between 9.00am and 12 noon operated between Washer Lane and Jubilee

Road bottom while the Halifax to Jubilee Road bottom via Bailey Hall and Swan Bank service was operated to Park Lane between these hours. From mid-December the Corporation began to fit a gadget, designed by the General Manager G.F.Craven, which comprised a 12in x 4in box with a glass panel above the platform to be seen by alighting passengers. The words 'Bus Moving' were illuminated in bright red letters when the bus was moving but died out as it stopped. This was intended to prevent numerous minor accidents in blackout when passengers were deceived by the speed of the bus. Considered to be of national importance, the cost of installation was approximately £1 per bus. Following an instruction by the Regional Traffic Commissioner, stopping places were reduced wherever possible without causing undue inconvenience to the travelling public on all Corporation services in a bid to save fuel and wear and tear on brakes and the JOC also made similar alterations on its services outside the Borough.

Following the sale by the Corporation of its 4 1932 vintage AEC Regals to the Ministry of War Transport in December 1941 for use by the Ministry of Supply, at the JOC meeting on 25 March 1942, provisional arrangements were made to provide 22 single deck buses (11 each from the Corporation and JOC) to be placed under the control of Northern Command in the event of invasion and it was stated that it would be necessary to enroll at least 64 drivers in the Home Guard. Additionally, in March 1942 three of the Corporation's AEC Regents were loaned to West Yorkshire Road Car Co. Ltd. whose need for additional vehicles arose from its requirement to supply a large number of buses for

Climbing Rochdale Road at Greetland whilst working a duty on the 55 service during the early years of World War II is Joint Omnibus Committee English Electric-bodied AEC Regent 139 (JX2039). Despite still wearing its pre-war orange, green & cream livery, it has been fitted with headlight masks and had its mudguard edges painted white while as can be clearly seen, white markings have also been applied to the topless lamp post, telegraph pole and wall corners.
T.Worsnop collection

With high walls having been built to protect the Halifax Building Society against enemy attacks, Corporation Park Royal-bodied AEC Regent no.10 (JX1788) with white tipped mudguards and a mask fitted to its nearside headlight picks up its passengers in Commercial Street before setting off on its journey to the General Hospital. The poster on the side of the bus proudly announces that no.10 was the first provincial bus to answer London's appeal for assistance on 22 October 1940. *T.W.Worsnop collection*

This wartime view of Commercial Street shows Corporation 1938 Roe-bodied AEC Regent 49 (JX6570) leaving the town centre on a 35A journey to Highroad Well. Painted in grey livery with brown bands, it additionally carries a white band at the lower edge of its rear panel and on its mudguards. *R.Needham collection*

Looking extremely drab in its wartime grey livery with brown bands, Corporation 16 (JX2301), a 1935 vintage Roberts-bodied AEC Regent, is seen in Commercial Street, Halifax in 1945 still with its wing edges etc. painted white.
R.Marshall collection

the daily transportation of essential war workers to ordnance factories within its operating area. The buses involved were 8, 9 & 116 (AMV482, MV3522 & CP9442), all of which were allocated to West Yorkshire's Bradford depot and were most often used on its 55 service from Bradford to Yeadon due to low bridges on several other of that companies routes.

It was decided by the JOC that from 1 April the issue of separate tickets and accounting for Borough area receipts on joint services be abolished. Because of the declining percentage of area receipts, the gross receipts from these from the year ending 31 March 1943 was to be arrived at by taking 17.05% of the gross receipts for each year with the proviso that if these rose by £28,900 over the datum figure of gross receipts for the year ended 31 March 1941 of £192,523, the percentage should be reduced to 16.05% and if they fell by £28,900 the percentage should be increased to 18.05% and pro rata for amounts less than £28,900 with an agreement for a review if there was a material change in circumstances. This was to apply to all JOC routes apart from the three affected by the Sowerby Bridge tram abandonment, Rishworth, Sowerby, Beech Road and Mill Bank from which the percentage contribution was to continue to be calculated separately. Also, on 6 May it was agreed by the Passenger Transport Committee to provide an alternative exit at the rear of Elmwood garage for use in case of emergency while on Whit Saturday 23 May 1942 the receipts from passengers carried on the Corporation and JOC services constituted a record since the inception of the municipal transport undertaking in Halifax in 1898.

After approving a change of termini at its meeting on 30 May 1942 for the following services :
Wheatley/Bradshaw from the top of Albion Street to the top of Westgate and the West End circular from Alexandra Street to Fountain Street near the Tuel Lane stand
in a bid to further save fuel and rubber, the following service alterations were implemented on 1 November :
(a) Last buses to leave the town termini each evening not later than 8.0pm.
(b) Sunday services reduced in aggregate by approximately 50%.
(c) Stopping places to be reduced further to not more than 4 stops per mile instead of 8.
(d) No services on Christmas Day, although this was later rescinded.

Protests were made to the Traffic Commissioner stating that, as well as the lack of prior consultation, these measures would create undue hardship owing to a lack of alternative means of transport and requesting instead a variation of the direction so as to provide for a percentage reduction of mileage. These were, however, decline.

Five Corporation buses were to be propelled by producer gas and were to be equipped to haul a trailer containing the apparatus for making gas, as required rather than from gas bag containers

TAKE A TIP FROM THE CAMEL!

Ride BETWEEN the Humps

8 AM   5 PM

AVOID CROWDED RUSH HOURS

One of a pair of Roe-bodied AEC Regents purchased in 1934 for the Corporation fleet, 12 (JX1912) in Rawson Street at the end of World War II still carries the white markings on its mudguards and rear panel which were applied for the blackout years.   *R.Marshall collection*

Painted in Halifax's wartime livery of grey with brown bands, Corporation Roe-bodied AEC Regent 64 (JX6897) was one of a number of buses converted to run on producer gas and is seen here in 1943 hauling a trailer on which the producer equipment was mounted.
T.Worsnop collection

on the top of buses. The Ministry of War Transport wished 16 buses to be thus adapted by July 1943 although it was generally felt that the area was unsuitable for such propulsion due to its numerous steep gradients. Additionally, the following bus termini were to be altered in order to achieve further savings :

Ovenden services 17/18/19/22 from Commercial Street to Waterhouse Street.

Wheatley and Bradshaw services 24/26 from Westgate to Crossley Street.

Copley service 27 from Wards End to Fountain Street bottom.

Outer Circle service 29 from Powell Street to the former Ovenden terminal at Commercial Street.

Boothtown, Claremount and Queensbury services 34/34A/59 from Union Street to Westgate.

The saving in mileage as a result of all the above measures was estimated to be 42,027 per year for Corporation services and 186,277 for those of the JOC.

Before 1942 ended, the Traffic Commissioner instructed that provision was to be made for transport for essential workers (Home Guard, Civil Defence, Munitions etc.) after 9.0pm and although the Council disapproved, it made arrangements for 12 'Priority Buses' to operate at 9.40pm on the Elland, Heptonstall, Hebden Bridge, Highroad Well, Boothtown, Ovenden, Sandbeds (Pellon), Siddal, Skircoat Green, Southowram, Sowerby Bridge and West End services and later also to Hipperholme. Additionally, on 2 November the Beechwood to Albert Road service was extended to Luddenden Foot at the morning and evening peak times of operation.

The gas-propelled buses finally made their debut on 3 March 1943 on the Outer Circle (West End - Savile Park) service after the conversion of AEC Regents 38/40/8/73 to operate on a mixture of 40% fuel and 60% gas which was produced by the burning of anthracite in the trailer unit. The buses thus adapted proved to be smoother running and quieter than either petrol or diesel buses and despite only having 90% of the performance of conventionally powered buses were easily able to negotiate gradients of 1 in 11 without difficulty in time keeping. Thus, on 10 March it was decided to purchase six additional producer gas trailers at a cost of £120 each for Corporation vehicles as well as two for the JOC. The cost of maintenance was, however, high and the total average cost of operation was 2.79d per mile as opposed to 2.55d per mile with conventional fuel. From the beginning of November the Regional Traffic Commissioner consented to the operation of a slight increase in mileage on weekdays and a considerable increase on Sundays from 7 November.

At a meeting of the Joint Omnibus Committee towards the end of 1943 it was agreed that if it did not press for new vehicles now, an assurance should be given that it should receive priority from the Ministry of Transport in its orders after the war. There had been a considerable increase in maintenance costs of 8-10 year-old vehicles and demand for new components and it would have required 34 double deckers and 12 single deckers for normal replacement purposes since September 1939 had

circumstances been normal. Although the 1935-39 vehicles were regarded as being capable for a further five years of service provided that spare parts were available, a provisional order was placed with AEC for 34 double and 12 single deckers for the JOC and 24 double and 6 single deckers for the Corporation. In the meantime, the 2 AEC Rangers (131/2) which had been sold to the Corporation for conversion to ambulances, were then reconverted to buses, sold to the LNE Railway Company and were repurchased by the JOC in 1942 and immediately placed in store, were converted to run on producer gas as were 3 AEC Regent double deckers. The 2 Rangers, however, were never used in their new form and remained in reserve until May 1945 when they were sold to a dealer.

Following a deputation to the Regional Traffic Commissioner being made on 28 January 1944 for buses to leave the town centre after 9.00pm which was supported by a petition from various Halifax trade and commerce organisations which contained 21,000 signatures, this matter was placed in the hands of the Ministry of War Transport for jurisdiction. The outcome was that additional fuel could not be allowed to run later services and that if it was felt that services should be extended even for a temporary period until 9.30 or 10.0pm, the transport department would have to effect a corresponding saving in mileage during normal hours without inconveniencing workpeople and shoppers. However, despite this ruling, the Traffic Commissioner was pressed to allow operation of buses up to 10.0pm daily on the following conditions :

(a) That evening services be curtailed on certain routes between 7.0pm and 9.0pm.

(b) That extra shopping services introduced on 1 November 1943 be withdrawn.

(c) That Sunday services be reduced by 10%.

This was submitted to the Traffic Commissioner with a protest against the use of their Emergency Powers never intended by those in authority. The request was turned down on 11 March because of the hardship to shoppers and those who wished to use Sunday services as well as the need to conserve vehicles and minimise operations during the blackout, with an additional indication that the Traffic Commissioner might need vehicles for workpeoples' services under the 1944 Production Programme involving large scale transfer of workers. This was received by the Passenger Transport Committee under protest. During this time, a partition wall had been built at Skircoat Road depot between the operating shed and the workshops while the additional exit had been provided at the rear of Elmwood garage as had previously been sanctioned.

By the end of September 1944 the obligation placed by the Ministry of War Transport on operators of large fleets of PSVs to operate a quota of their vehicles on producer gas had now been lifted with additional fuel being made available to cover the vehicles previously converted. Thus, around 15 of the Corporation and JOC's buses were able to be altered back to their original form of propulsion. From 6 November the Corporation and JOC were granted powers to operate later buses up to 10.0pm on

Mondays to Saturdays, subject to the duties and timetable being approved by the Commissioner and the same frequency was to operate between 9.0pm and 10.0pm as that between 8.0pm and 9.0pm with 'Priority Buses' ceasing.

Fortunately, whilst the works of such manufacturers as Crossley and Daimler suffered severe bomb damage during the dark war years the Southall premises of AEC were not affected in this way, and so whilst spares parts were not exactly plentiful, Halifax was able to maintain its fleet with slightly fewer problems than many other undertakings. In addition to maintaining its own vehicles, the Skircoat Road workshops also assisted a number of other undertakings including Kingston-upon-Hull and Wallasey Corporations by repairing several of their buses which had been damaged by enemy action.

The first major step towards the reinstatement of services after the ending of hostilities was an application at the end of August 1945 to the Regional Traffic Commissioner for the reintroduction of all pre-war bus stops while on 19 September the Passenger Transport Committee applied for a 15-minute circular bus service via Ovenden Road, Nursery Lane and Ovenden Way and vice versa in place of the existing service terminating in Nursery Lane. Additionally, an application was also made for an allocation of 25 RT-type AEC Regent III buses for the Joint Omnibus Committee and 25 for the Corporation in accordance with arrangements being made by the Ministry of Transport for the allocation of buses to passenger transport undertakings throughout the country. Although no new buses had been delivered to either the Corporation or JOC since March 1940, neither had any been withdrawn from service since this date until August 1945 when three of the JOC's 1933 AEC Regals were taken out of service. During the final month of the year two of the three AEC Regents loaned to West Yorkshire Road Car Co. Ltd. returned home and rejoined the Corporation fleet leaving only the third bus of this type and the two JOC Leyland Cubs still absent.

A RETURN TO PEACE

With peace having now returned to Britain, plans were laid for a return to normal bus operations in Halifax and its surrounds as well as the acquisition of new buses with which to replace the pre-war fleet that had given yeoman service through difficult times with the minimum of maintenance except that which was essential. One of the first developments resulted from a meeting on 17 January 1946 at Boulderclough Sunday School when negotiations for an extension of the bus service from Church Stile, Sowerby to High Lee Green, Boulderclough, a distance of one and a half miles, met with an unfavourable reply with the Halifax General Manager recommending a limited service to Shield Hall Lane bottom, a distance of only half a mile. Sowerby Bridge District Council requested a further inspection of the route by the Joint Omnibus Committee and following this, agreed on 6 February to make passing places, a turning place and put the road into a reasonable state of repair.

Upon learning in January that Frank Garside of West Vale Garage wished to dispose of his business, the JOC on 28 February made a bid of £2,500 for its purchase which included his service between West Vale and Dean Head via Saddleworth Road and a 1935 vintage 26-seat Bedford WTL coach, subject to his agreement not to operate any stage carriage service within the area of the JOC. Following the completion of the deal the JOC assumed operation of Garside's service on 7 June and although the Bedford coach was taken over, it was not operated by its new owner and was immediately sold for £560.

Requests were received from residents in several areas for post boxes, withdrawn from buses at the start of the war, to be restored but these were refused by the Post Office as part of its new post-war policy. Meanwhile it was hoped that from 15 April, when summer time commenced, to operate later buses, the aim being for a speedy return to pre September 1939 schedules. Because of the difficult labour position, however, it was felt that this might not be achievable in one step and although permission was granted with last departures up to 11.0pm on weekdays and Saturdays and 10.0pm on Sundays, as a result of objections from the Trade Union these did not commence until 20 May. Due to running at a loss and the difficulty in recruiting suitable boys of 16/17 years of age, it was decided to discontinue the parcels delivery service from 31 August and to close the parcels department. A further reason for its abandonment was the fact that parcels were apparently causing platform accidents and hindering conductors in their collection of fares.

At around this same time, the Traffic Commissioner refused consent on grounds of the unsuitability of certain sections of routes in the town centre to the operation of buses of 8ft. width, a type in which the Corporation and JOC had already expressed an interest despite them not yet being generally available. The Commissioner did, however, agree to their operation on the Halifax - Huddersfield, Halifax - Brighouse via Slead Syke and Bonegate and Halifax - Hebden Bridge services and as a result 16 buses of the 54 on order for the JOC were altered to be of this dimension at an extra cost of £50 each. The purchase was sanctioned by the Corporation but not without dissent since tenders were not invited for these vehicles and the cost of their bodies (£1,734 for 8ft width double deck, £1,684 for 7ft.6in width double deck and £1,222 for single deck) was considered to be exorbitant although this price had to be paid to avoid the possibility of getting wet timber frames. By now, the last of the three AEC Regents had been returned from West Yorkshire Road Car Co. Ltd. in March followed by the two Leyland Cubs from the LNE Railway Company in April, although neither of the latter re-entered service in Halifax and were instead placed in store.

On 20 October the circular bus service between Washer Lane and Jubilee Road bottom, Siddal was discontinued and instead the service from town to Washer Lane was made into an independent circular route while an augmented service was run to Park Lane, Siddal. During the middle of the following month consent was obtained to extend the present Mill Bank service from the Alma Inn to Pleasant View at Lightazles Road, a distance of 340 yards, following pressure from Ripponden District Council as a result of a local petition. Later in the year the JOC

The first post-war buses to be received by the Corporation were Roe-bodied AEC Regent IIIs with London Transport RT-type chassis which arrived in 1946. One of these, 35 (JX9406) travels along St.James Road, Halifax in 1958 on JOC route 48 to Hebden Bridge. *J.Fozard*

applied for permission to operate a works service to Bowers Mill, Barkisland for an experimental period and although this was ultimately granted, it did not, in fact, commence operation until April 1947.

The first of the long-awaited new buses (306 : JX9406) arrived in Halifax in November 1946 and gave a demonstration run on 5 December on the department's stiffest climb, a section of the Greetland route from West Vale, its passengers including General Managers from all the principal municipal undertakings in the West Riding of Yorkshire. An AEC Regent III of London Transport's RT-type with a low profile bonnet and radiator and powered by a 9.6 litre engine, it was fitted with a 56-seat Roe bodywork and looked superb in Halifax's attractive orange, green and cream colours. After entering service on the Huddersfield route, 306 was joined by 7 more buses of this combination (301-5/7/8 : JX9401-5/7/8), all of which were placed in service by the Corporation before the end of 1946. Almost immediately, however, 4 of them (305-8) were transferred to the JOC fleet and given new fleet numbers 209-12. The arrival of these new buses enabled a similar number of pre-war AEC Regents to be taken out of service but, following a request for assistance from Sheffield Corporation who was short of buses due to delays in the delivery of new vehicles, rather than dispose of these they were dispatched on loan to the city of steel. In total, 6 Corporation and 2 JOC Regents travelled south and gave their new temporary operator several months of valuable service before returning to Halifax during the summer of the following year.

1947 began with the announcement that the Halifax's General Manager G.F.Craven had been awarded the OBE in the New Year's Honours List, this being for services to public transport. This was a fitting reward for a person who had given so much to the bus industry in general as well as to Halifax and its surrounds. Not withstanding this, however, Mr.Craven signalled his intention to retire on 13 August and thus the wheels were set in motion to find his replacement. After considering a number of applicants, F.E.Cook, General Manager & Engineer of Southport Corporation was appointed on 2 June and took up his position as Halifax General Manager on 1 September.

The heavy snow falls during February 1947 wreaked havoc on bus services over a large part of Britain and Halifax was no exception. With its steep hills and rural surrounds, it was deemed necessary to operate buses in pairs on some routes in case of mishap in deep snow and even so, buses had to be abandoned at Heptonstall, Outlane, Dean Head and Causeway Foot as a result of drifting. The Passenger Transport Committee meanwhile, on 19 February, resolved to introduce increased services on all routes as soon as the labour position improved and acknowledged that the Ovenden services in particular had been difficult to maintain at certain times of the day.

Despite no further new buses having been received, two more of the JOC's pre-war AEC Regents were loaned to Sheffield Corporation in February to assist it during its difficulties while back in Halifax disaster struck on Easter Monday 7 April when fully laden Corporation Regent no.4 (JX323) overturned at the Calder & Hebble Inn, Salterhebble while working a relief journey on the Halifax - Huddersfield route. The cause of the accident was believed to be a broken spring which made the steering uncontrollable. A total of 37 passengers were injured including 4 who had to be detained in hospital whilst the bus was severely damaged with its roof torn away and all its windows smashed. Although it was not repaired due to its age, its chassis was retained by the Corporation and after being fitted with a lorry body it survived in use for a further three years. Later in April, 4 of the Corporation's 1937 Park Royal-bodied AEC Regents were sold to Nottingham City Transport for £1,500 each and were repainted into their new owner's green and cream livery at the Corporation's Skircoat Road workshops before their departure. Soon afterwards, the buses which had been on loan to Sheffield Corporation began to return home with the last arriving in July.

Due to the late delivery of its new buses and increased service demands, the JOC expanded its fleet from 73 to 80 vehicles by retaining 7 buses scheduled for disposal. The policy was now to dispose of the vehicles in the worst condition first rather than by age and thus a number of the single and double deckers dating from 1933/4 were given an extension to their lives. Their replacements, AEC Regent IIIs with Park Royal bodywork (217-26 : ACP401-10) began to arrive in October, however, and were all in service before the end of December thus enabling the mass withdrawal of pre-war members of the fleet. The Corporation also received a number of new buses at this same time and although 9 were similar Park Royal-bodied AEC Regent IIIs (309-17 : ACP414-22), the remainder were Leyland PD2/1s fitted with handsome Leyland bodies (335-41 : ACP384-90). Unlike the AECs which had pre-selector gearboxes and air brakes, the Leylands were fitted with 4-speed synchromesh boxes and vacuum servo brakes and were thus less popular with drivers, particularly on the Corporation's more hilly routes.

A service which surprisingly began on 8 December, having previously been rejected by the Council, was that which ran along

Seen on 9 July 1947 whilst on loan to Sheffield Corporation is Halifax JOC English Electric-bodied AEC Regent 140 (JX2040). Upon its return to its rightful owner later that month, it continued to give service to the citizens of Halifax for a further eleven months before being withdrawn and sold in June 1948. *R.Marshall collection*

Masking one of the 1946 RT-type AEC Regent IIIs, Corporation 86 (JX7056), a 1939 Weymann-bodied AEC Regent, collects its Northowram-bound passengers in Halifax town centre in the late 'forties. *T.Worsnop collection*

Taking a rest in Powell Street, Halifax before undertaking its next journey on service 29A to Albert Road in July 1952 is Corporation Roe-bodied AEC Regent III 307 (ACP633) which a few weeks later was renumbered 55.
R.Marshall collection

Ramsden Street, Wheatley to Bank Edge Road, Cousin Lane to serve a new housing development in the area. Additionally, in the middle of the month frequencies were increased on routes in the Ryburn Valley on weekdays whilst the Greetland and Hebden Bridge services were increased on Saturdays and most JOC routes had their frequencies improved on Sundays. At this same time the operation of double deck buses on the Warley and Washer Lane services was approved and the Corporation fleet was fixed at 82 double deck and 5 single deck vehicles for more effective operation.

As a consequence of the Transport Act 1947, from 1 January 1948 the British Transport Commission delegated to the Railway Executive certain functions relating to the activities of the Railway Companies transferred to the Commission. As far as it affected the Joint Omnibus Committee, the following arrangements were to be made : Advertising and publicity matters were to be undertaken by Halifax Corporation and British Railways; Agreements and formal documents - Halifax Corporation and the Railway Executive; Vehicles - Halifax Corporation and British Railways, and the name of the Railway Executive instead of the individual companies was to be placed on the vehicles in railway ownership.

Following the receipt of 4 more new AEC Regent IIIs with Roe bodies (213-6 : ACP627-30) and 3 with Park Royal bodies (227-9 : ACP411-3) by the JOC and 4 Park Royal (318-21 : ACP423-6) and 4 Roe-bodied Regent IIIs (305-8 : ACP631-4) together with another 2 all-Leyland PD2/1s (342/3 : ACP391/2) by the Corporation between January and March 1948, the Corporation decided to sell for the first time by auction 35 buses (including 6 JOC vehicles) now surplus to requirements which were well maintained and in running order. This produced £12,000, with the

historic 1934 AEC Regent no.10, the first provincial bus to operate in London in October 1940 achieving a bid of £460, 33 buses dating from 1932-5 being sold for between £120 and £520 each and 2 1937 buses attaining £1,000 each.

In a bid to relieve serious congestion in Halifax town centre, on 7 April the Town Council passed a resolution to move 'outside bus companies' stands from Albion Street and Carrier Street to the south of Union Street and Horton Street, although it was suggested that Woolshops would be a better location. In conjunction with this, a number of the stands used by JOC and Corporation services were to be altered but as a result of objections being received by the Traffic Commissioner it was decided to deal with the matter at a public sitting. On the same day the JOC informed Sowerby Bridge Urban District Council that permission had been granted for the Boulderclough service, subject to the Council providing turning facilities at the junction of Shield Hall Lane, but due to the time taken to complete this work the service, which was an extension of that to the Beechwood Estate, did not commence until 15 September. An application was made by the JOC to operate a service from Brighouse to Stoney Lane to serve the new Smith House, Summerfield and Stoney Lane housing developments while the Corporation applied to extend the existing service 29A (Sandbeds via Pellon New Road) from the junction of Rye Lane and Sandbeds to the junction of Rye Lane and Ryecroft Lane. It was not now necessary for the Railway Executive to hold licences for the services operated by it and the Corporation and thus in future these would be held in the name of the Corporation only, although the cost was still chargeable to the Joint Omnibus Committee.

On the day of the JOC meeting on 29 June, the 50th anniversary of the public commencement of Halifax's tramway

Seen in post-war years after having its original half-drop windows replaced with sliding ventilators, Corporation Roe-bodied AEC Regent 13 (JX6894) awaits its departure to Ovenden Road on the 17A service. Its crew meanwhile enjoy a brief break from their duties.
R.Marshall collection

Typifying the Halifax double decker of the 1947-50 period, Park Royal-bodied AEC Regent III 346 (AJX372) illustrates the thin pillar styling favoured by the undertaking during the early post-war years. It is seen here at Broad Street, Halifax in April 1963 prior to working a journey to Cousin Lane on route 9.
R.Marshall

Travelling along Waterhouse Street, Halifax on its way to West End is Corporation all-Leyland PD2/1 101 (ACP385) which dated from 1947. Sold in January 1966 to Oldham Corporation, it gave its new owner a further three years service before being disposed of for scrap in February 1969. *R.F.Mack*

system was celebrated by the undertaking and to this end members of the Corporation and JOC Committees after taking lunch at the White Swan Hotel enjoyed a circular run in buses around the district in the afternoon before sitting down to tea at Hebden Bridge.

Between April and August a further 18 new Park Royal-bodied AEC Regent IIIs arrived and were placed in service with 13 (322-34 : ACP800-3/915-23) joining the Corporation fleet and 5 (230-4 : ACP795-9) being for use by the JOC. To allow for an increase in fleet size from 75 to 87 buses and meet the present day traffic requirements, the JOC instead of withdrawing 18 buses from service following the receipt of their replacements, retained 12 supernumerary vehicles (9 double deckers and 3 single deckers) for this purpose. The Corporation, meanwhile, sold 4 of its surplus 1938 vintage AEC Regents (40/7-9) to Rochdale Corporation in whose fleet they gave up to five more years of service.

Having continued to use Bell Punch rack-type tickets since the early tramway days, it was thought that the time had come to investigate more modern ticket systems and in order to evaluate some of the types on offer, an Ultimate machine was trialed by the JOC between 13 July and 15 August and similarly a TIM machine was evaluated for a period commencing 25 August. Following these experiments it was decided on 16 February 1949 to adopt the Ultimate system on 'A' services and to this end 170 machines were ordered on rental terms. A saving in administrative costs of £4000 was expected, with an estimated 50% saving in time in the issuing of tickets. The existing Bell Punch tickets were, however, to be retained on 'B' services, although their conversion to a single box was expected to save £2032 per annum.

On 20 October 1948, the Passenger Transport Committee took the decision to operate, subject to consent, Sunday morning skeleton services of 60 minutes headway on the following routes : 17/17A Ovenden Circular; 20 Causeway Foot; 21 Wainstalls; 22 Mixenden; 24 Wheatley; 26 Bradshaw; 27 Copley; 27A Warley; 28 Norton Tower; 29 Pellon/Savile Park; 30 Southowram; 31 General Hospital and 34A Claremount and on a 30 minute headway to Siddal (23) and Highroad Well (35A). No JOC services were thus affected at this time.

The first ever 8ft wide buses in the fleet, Park Royal-bodied AEC Regent IIIs 235-45 (AJX361-71) entered service on 1 December 1948 on the Huddersfield, Brighouse and Hebden Bridge routes of the JOC whilst the remainder of the batch (246-50 : AJX372-6) took up their duties a month later on 1 January

1949. Of the buses these replaced, two were retained as supernumerary to accommodate the increase in traffic at peak hours and with the vehicle required for use on the new Stoney Lane service from Brighouse which commenced on 6 December, the fleet strength of the JOC was increased from 87 to 90. After the first day of operation of the new service, however, the single decker intended for its maintenance was replaced by a double decker which then became the customary type.

Three days before Christmas, it was learned that it had now become necessary to make safe the roof of the Skircoat Road depot owing to the settlement of the foundations of the attached office buildings and at this same time the Passenger Transport Committee approved in principle the establishment of a bus station at Crossfield which would include the provision for 35 routes (including those of other operators), particularly those that were through services and certain of those running north and west bound. Provision was also included in the plan for waiting rooms, snack bar and an enquiry office. This was, however, subject to the approval of the Ministry of Transport as well as that of the Home Office in respect of the demolition of air raid shelters under the site. The plan, in general, was authorised by the Town Council at its meeting on 5 January 1949 subject to modifications in that it would cater for all vehicles entering the town from North Bridge, Lee Bridge, Pellon Lane, Hanson Lane and Gibbet Street. As the Corporation operated 60 routes and Hebble and Yorkshire Woollen District 15, at least two bus stations were needed to accommodate them, one on the north side of the town, the other on the south side. Measuring approximately 5,000 sq.yards, the Crossfield site was the only one available with sufficient accommodation without the need for property demolition although the slope of the area and the underground air raid shelters presented major difficulties and it was agreed that a further site be found on the south side when the opportunity arose. The layout planned for the new bus station was easily adaptable to changing route patterns, however, and would comply with the ring road scheme already approved by the Council. The approval of the Ministry was eventually gained on 24 August 1949, although this stated that all buses should enter the new bus station via its highest level and depart from its lowest point via Great Albion Street. Meanwhile, it was not until this same date that permission was given by the Council for the re-roofing of Skircoat Road depot at a cost of £12,266 which included using high tensile steel wherever possible.

On 26 January 1949 approval was given for the crest of the JOC on the side of its buses to be altered to have the Halifax coat of arms with the words 'Halifax Joint Committee', thus removing all reference to the railway companies which had in 1948 been nationalised under the title of British Railways. The transformation of the JOC fleet was undertaken quickly and the old crest had disappeared completely by the early part of March. Following this move, in May 1949 Alderman Gledhill, who had been instrumental in the formation of the JOC, retired after serving on the Committee since November 1927.

At an inquiry held on 9 June into the proposed transfer of the bus stands of Hebble Motor Services and Yorkshire Woollen District from Albion Street and Westgate to Horton Street and Union Street it was proposed that of the eleven services using

Albion Street, four would remain as would one of the four in Carrier Street and four of the five in Westgate with all the others being moved to Horton Street and Union Street. This, however, brought objections from A.Pulman & Sons on account of bad access to their premises in Union Street and congestion in Horton Street, particularly for long vehicles carrying girders and other structural materials. Despite this, approval for these changes was received from the Ministry of Transport in mid-July for the removal of three bus stands to each of Horton Street and Union Street for company vehicles!

The first new single deck bus since before the war entered service in June in the form of a rear entrance AEC Regal III for the JOC. Numbered 255 (AJX845), this was joined by identical 251-4/6-62 (AJX841-4/6-52) at the beginning of July, enabling a similar number of pre-war AEC Regal single deckers to be withdrawn and sold. Later in the year, more new Roe-bodied AEC Regal III single deckers were received of which 1 each were placed in service by the JOC and Corporation in November with a further 6 joining the JOC example in December and at this same time 4 more making their debut with the Corporation.

The start of the new decade brought the approval of the Passenger Transport Committee on 18 January 1950 of a new hourly service from the town centre to Gleanings Avenue, Paddock Lane and Norton Tower, but only at the expense of the Tuel Lane (Beech Road) route which was reduced to an hourly frequency. This was only agreed after a previous resolution for refusal had been referred back by the Town Council because people were promised a service in 1939 when the houses were built and it was over 1,000 ft above sea level with no protection against the elements. On 10 March, the JOC decided to introduce Ultimate ticket issuing machines on its services and as a consequence 170 of these machines were obtained on rental. Concurrent with this decision was the approval for the operation of one bus in the peak periods from the Travellers Rest Inn on the Midgley route to Booth, subject to Sowerby Bridge Urban District Council providing a turning point. This being accomplished, the service began on 26 June.

The last Park Royal-bodied AEC Regent IIIs of 7ft.6in width entered service in the JOC fleet at the beginning of April 1950 (270-83 : BCP664-77) and indeed also were its last new buses for a period of four years. Their arrival not only further modernised the fleet but also enabled a quantity of the pre-war double deckers to be withdrawn and sold. Although the Corporation did not benefit from any new buses during 1950, in November of the following year it received 6 East Lancs-bodied Daimler CD650 double deckers (349-54 : CCP601-6) which were easily distinguishable by their wide, polished radiators. Fitted with 10.62 litre engines, these were powerful vehicles which made easy work of the many steep hills around Halifax and with power steering and pre-selector gearboxes they proved popular with the driving staff. A month later these were joined by 5 of a batch of 6 Park Royal-bodied AEC Regent IIIs (355-9 : CCP607-11), the sixth example (360 : CCP612) taking up its duties on 1 January 1952.

Sadly, at home at lunchtime on 10 October 1951 the General Manager & Engineer F.E.Cook died suddenly at the young age of 46 and as a temporary measure, the former holder of this post, G.F.Craven, offered to carry out the managerial duties without

While a number of the Roe-bodied AEC Regal IIIs purchased by the Joint Omnibus Committee in 1949 were later converted to front entrance layout, 255 (AJX845) retained its porch-type rear entrance until its withdrawal and sale in 1962. Seen at the Crossfield bus station parking area at Gt.Albion Street in 1960, it still looked smart in its original-style orange, green & cream livery.
T.Worsnop collection

Pre and post-war AEC Regents rub shoulders at Wards End, Halifax in 1952. Both looking immaculate, Corporation 14 (JX6895) is a 1938 Roe-bodied bus while JOC 274 (BCP668) carries a Park Royal body and dates from 1950.   *R.Marshall*

salary until a successor was appointed. This was accepted with much gratitude by the Passenger Transport Committee. On 27 November 1951, Roderick MacKenzie was appointed as the undertaking's new General Manager & Engineer and took up his post on 2 February 1952. Previously Divisional Engineer of British Road Services in Birmingham, he had, however, a wide experience of bus operation having earlier served with Edinburgh Corporation before becoming General manager of Warrington Passenger Transport Department.

Following a survey of its operations, the JOC revealed in January 1952 that losses were being incurred on the Elland - Triangle; Halifax -Heptonstall; Halifax - Hullen Edge; Elland - Norland; Elland - Outlane; Halifax - Mill Bank; Cragg Vale - Mytholmroyd; Ripponden - Elland and West Vale - Dean Head services and as a consequence it was decided to discontinue the Elland - Outlane and Elland - Norland routes and revise the Elland - Triangle; Halifax - Outlane and Halifax - Hullen Edge services. Thus, on 25 August the portion of the Elland-Triangle route which operated along South Lane and Savile Road was withdrawn and its terminus relocated to the junction of Huddersfield Road and Dewsbury Road, Elland instead of Catherine Street while the frequency of the Hullen Edge route was reduced. Additionally, the Elland - Outlane service was replaced by a new service from

Halifax to Holywell Green and the number of journeys on the Halifax - Outlane service was increased to compensate. Later in the year, part of the Midgley service on Saturday afternoons was transferred to Booth to give a 30 minute service to the former and 60 minute frequency to the latter from the start of November while on 17 December it was decided to split the Tuel Lane (Beech Road) and Paddock Lane service and to adjust the Paddock Lane portion.

On the vehicle front, a dual-door, underfloor-engined Daimler Freeline single decker was borrowed from its manufacturer for evaluation from 12 October and was put to work on the Huddersfield route. Complaints that its 30 seat plus 30 standing layout provided insufficient seating were addressed later that same week by increasing its capacity to 36 seats plus 12 standing and after its initial period of operation it was transferred to other routes. This was followed early in 1953 by a Gardner-engined Guy Arab III which was borrowed from Lancashire United Transport and this too was trialled on a number of different routes. In the event, neither of these buses produced orders for their manufacturers after being found less than suited to Halifax's terrain. Of the existing fleet, Corporation no.28 (JX7047), a 1939 AEC Regent, was converted to a breakdown wagon and took up its new role in December.

Proving that there is life after passenger carrying service, the Corporation's 1939 AEC Regent JX7047 had its double deck Roe body replaced in 1952 by a wagon body prior to giving a further twelve years of service as the undertaking's recovery wagon. It is seen here in Crossfield bus station during the late 'fifties bearing ancillary fleet no. 405.
T.Worsnop collection

ONE MAN OPERATION

Despite having introduced one-man-operated buses in the mid-1920s, crew operation had been the norm in Halifax since the early 'thirties and it was not until January 1953 that one-man-operation was restarted on an experimental basis. For this purpose, one of the Joint Omnibus Committee's Roe-bodied AEC Regal III single deckers was rebuilt from rear to front entrance configuration for use on the Mytholmroyd - Cragg Vale route. After gaining experience with this and finding it to be successful, a further 13 of the 1949 AEC Regal IIIs were similarly rebuilt and other routes such as those to Dean Head and Elland - Ripponden were thus changed to this method of operation. Soon afterwards, an application was made by the JOC during February for a Countryside Tour which included Booth, Midgley, Old Town, Hebden Bridge, Mytholmroyd, Cragg Vale, Blackstone Edge and Steep Lane, Sowerby, this being granted in time for its operation to start on Whit Sunday 24 May with a fare of 2/6d for adults and 1/9d for children. This was operated by the AEC Regal IIIs which had been converted for one-man-operation, some of which were later repainted in a predominantly cream livery with orange waistband and green roof. At around this same time. and as part of Roderick MacKenzie's search for economy, the standard bus livery was modified to a simpler application with orange lower and green upper panels and cream window surrounds, this being applied to both the Corporation and JOC fleets as vehicles became due for repainting.

To commemorate the Coronation of H.M.Queen Elizabeth II, 1938 vintage Park Royal-bodied AEC Regent 22 (JX6931) was specially decorated and ran from 28 May to 6 June, albeit not in passenger service but on both Corporation and JOC services each afternoon and evening. The design was produced by the Halifax School of Art and was applied jointly by the school and the Passenger Transport Department. Following its use in this unusual role, it returned to its normal revenue-earning duties which it continued until its final withdrawal from service in 1954.

Meanwhile, plans for the proposed new bus station at Crossfield crept a stage further when on 24 July it was announced that its cost had been reduced from £35,000 to £30,000 by the deletion of the 3 stands in Gt.Albion Street which reduced the total number from 21 to 18. Sanction was given by the Ministry of Transport for this revised plan, subject to certain economies in the lighting.

On 21 October 1953 Hepton Rural District Council, after unsuccessful talks with Todmorden Corporation, formally approached the JOC with a request for a single deck service to New Bridge, Hardcastle Crags via Lees Road and Midgehole Road to cater for the needs both of residents and visitors to the area. This brought an immediate and positive response and an application was speedily made by the JOC to run such a service from Hebden Bridge in conjunction with the Cragg Vale - Mytholmroyd route and this commenced on 12 July.

Resting in Powell Street, Halifax in June 1954 soon after it had been converted from rear to front entrance to make it suitable for one-man-operation, JOC Roe-bodied AEC Regal III 257 (AJX847) had also gained a predominantly cream livery at this same time.
R.Marshall

As 1953 drew to a close, due to the increasing losses incurred in the current financial year (£30,000), the Passenger Transport Committee resolved on 16 December to apply for the elimination of workmen's fares on the services of both the Corporation and the JOC as this would result in a saving of £14,000 per year on 'A' services and a similar amount on 'B' services in a full year. This was ratified by the Town Council on 8 January 1954 and agreed by the JOC two days later, although there was strong opposition to this plan, particularly from the Halifax Trades Council. The alternative was to raise fares all round or obtain a rate in aid of public transport and ultimately fare and stage revisions were chosen. Coincidental with this, an application was made for a second Countryside Tour covering Rooley Lane, Plain Lane, Rotten Row Road, Otter Lee Lane, Salt Drake Lane (Sowerby), Clay Pitts Lane (Ripponden), Causeway Head, Blue Ball Road, Rochdale Road, Baitings Gate Road, Long

Awaiting its departure to Halifax at Southowram terminus in July 1955, Corporation Park Royal-bodied AEC Regent III 67 (ACP921) was one of around forty buses to be repainted in MacKenzie-style livery with cream window surrounds. *R.Marshall*

Westgate, Halifax is the setting for this view of Corporation Park Royal-bodied AEC Regent III 320 (ACP425) which was about to depart for Northowram on route 32A in April 1951. As can be seen, it was fitted with an experimental style of destination screen which was obviously instigated by the new General Manager, Roderick MacKenzie and was based on the style favoured by several of the major operators in Scotland.
R.Marshall

Corporation East Lancs-bodied Daimler CD650 86 (CCP606) which was new in 1951 and is seen a few years later in Orange Street, Halifax later and Park Royal-bodied AEC Regent III 356 (CCP608) standing outside the Halifax Building Society in Commercial Street whilst working route 29 to West End in the early summer of 1952 both typify the MacKenzie era by being fitted with Scottish style destination indicators.
T.Worsnop collection/R.Marshall

Causeway, Commons and Rishworth, but an objection was made by the West Riding County Council on the grounds that the roads concerned in Soyland and Ripponden were too narrow and tortuous. Despite this, however, the application was subsequently granted and Tour No.2 started on 2 May with the adult fare of 2/6d and child fare of 1/3d. Both the Countryside Tours were of 24 miles length and operated on Sundays and at holiday times with seats being able to be booked in advance. Meanwhile, on 22 March the JOC Tuel Lane (Beech Road) and Corporation Claremount services were linked, although because of different

control through fares could not be introduced.

The first new buses to be received since 1951 made their debut in February 1954 when the Corporation placed in service 12 Roe-bodied Daimler CVG6 double deckers fitted with Gardner 6LW engines (87-98 : DCP831-42). These were followed in July and August by 10 buses of the same type but fitted with Metro Cammell double deck bodywork for the JOC (284-93 : DCP843-52) and these new arrivals allowed the withdrawal of all but three of the remaining pre-war AEC Regents from both fleets. By now, most of the early post-war Park Royal-bodied AEC Regent IIIs were suffering badly from the penny-pinching of their body specification. Bought at a time when the price of new buses was continually rising and new vehicles were being acquired via monetary loans, to save on costs window pans were deleted from the specification and instead the timber main frames were rebated to take the glass. As a result of this together with very thin window pillars and some dubious post war timber, a substantial amount of repair and rebuilding work had now become necessary if these buses were to continue in service, whereas the Roe-bodied examples with their sturdy teak frames did not suffer in this way, nor did the Leyland Titans bought for comparison.

On Sunday 29 August the long-awaited new bus station at Crossfield became operational, much to the consternation of traders and shoppers alike, with the services using it from the north travelling via New Broad Street and those from the south via Cow Green. In less than a month, however, it was decided that the Claremount - Beech Road service should be removed from the new bus station and resume its former route through the markets area of the town to give better access for shoppers while the transfer of other services from their town centre termini to Crossfield precipitated the formation of the Halifax Town Centre Traders Association to take action as a result of the loss of trade suffered and organise, together with the Chamber of Trade, petitions from traders and shoppers which culminated with 9,000

signatures being obtained. This also resulted in a proposal to extend the bus station by using land on the north side of the site, formerly occupied by St.James Church, being withdrawn before the 7 October meeting of the Town Council. Additionally, the Halifax Trades Council urged the Passenger Transport Committee to inaugurate a bus service from Halifax railway station to the bus station via Horton Street and Cow Green, returning by means of Broad Street, Winding Road and Square Road. Although the Committee did not accede fully to this request, for a trial period it re-routed the Boothtown and

Queensbury services on inward journeys to the bus station via Crossley Street and Waterhouse Street from 15 November 1954 and allowed Hebble's service from Bradford to Halifax via Queensbury to do the same. The Siddal service was also to be extended to the bus station via Horton Street, Fountain Street, Bull Green and Cow Green from 3 January 1955, returning via Gt.Albion Street, Waterhouse Street, Commercial Street and Horton Street. As the suggested town centre service would involve 130,000 extra miles per year with 4 more buses and 10 additional staff at a cost of £13,700 without corresponding revenue, this was accordingly rejected. Permission was, however, granted for the revision of the West End services as well as the linking of the Newlands/Warley - Bradshaw services and the re-routing of the Beech Road - Claremount service via the markets area and these became effective from 25 October 1954. Later, on 6 December, the West vale - Dean Head and Elland - Ripponden services were linked together with a coordinated timetable.

During December 1954, G.G.Hilditch, a man whose name was to later become synonymous with Halifax and who had previously been employed by Manchester Corporation Transport as Technical Assistant, was appointed as Assistant Engineer at Halifax. As will be seen in the following chapters, his influence was responsible for numerous changes in the town's bus operations and the choice of vehicles for both the Corporation and JOC fleets.

Shortly before the year ended, the number of buses required by the JOC reduced and as a result 6 of its AEC Regent IIIs (4 Roe-bodied RT types and 2 Park Royal-bodied examples) were transferred to the Corporation with the Roe-bodied buses thus 'returning home'.

Because of the continuous increase in the cost of operating its bus services and the need to introduce every reasonable economy, a special meeting was held by the Passenger Transport Committee on 26 January 1955 to review all the facilities provided by the Passenger Transport Department. Due to the adverse reaction to the service and frequency variations of the previous year and consequent inconvenience to passengers, it was decided that there should be no further curtailment of services and to provide additional facilities on the Wainstalls (21), Siddal (23), Newlands (26) and General Hospital (31) routes and to restore the West End (29/31) services to their pre-October 1954 route with effect from 21 February. To avoid crossing the dangerous Wrigley Hill into Whitehill Road, Illingworth, it was agreed to replace the Illingworth (Moor Chapel) and School Lane services with an equivalent service operating along Illingworth Road and Occupation Lane, returning via Whitehill Road. The Wheatley service was also to be extended to the junction of Hollins Road and Mixenden Road in order to serve the new housing developments in the area.

During the week commencing 21 February 1955, an experiment with a partially unpainted bus took place in order to establish whether or not repair costs could be reduced. The vehicle concerned - 1950 AEC Regent III 282 (BCP676) - was fitted with panels of bright aluminium with a light stucco finish to conceal surface blemish and damage more effectively on what

were formerly orange painted panels. If the experiment had been successful, it was intended that these panels were to be used on the whole of the vehicle rather than only those below the lower deck windows, but in the event the idea was quickly rejected and 282 was restored to its original state.

Despite Crossfield bus station having been in use since August 1954, it was not until 16 May 1955 that the 'official opening' ceremony was performed, this being undertaken by the Mayor of Halifax, Alderman N.E.Barber JP who unfolded a Union Jack to reveal a 28in x 16in bronze plaque with enamel lettering. Officialdom works in unusual, and often slow, ways! During this same month the end of yet another era was reached when Charles Holdsworth, one of the founders of Hebble Bus Services, finally retired from the Town Council after serving on the Passenger Transport and its previous committees for 26 years.

Already looking ahead, applications were made by the Corporation and JOC to add a further three Countryside Tours to the existing two for the 1956 season, although in the event this was refused by the traffic commissioner on 28 November whilst earlier on 25 September 1955 one-man-operation was introduced on the Elland - Triangle (41), Norland (56) and Copley (27) services on Sundays using the cream-liveried AEC Regal III single deckers. Proposals were also made for the linking of certain services to remove congestion in Waterhouse Street and Crossley Street under which the Beechwood Road service would be joined to the Stainland and Outlane routes using the bus station, Waterhouse Street and Commercial Street and returning via Commercial Street, Waterhouse Street, Orange Street and Corporation Street. Surprisingly, however, there would be no through fares with passengers having to re-book when they reached Waterhouse Street although through fares were made available on the linked Hebden Bridge - Brighouse service when this was introduced on 3 October. Meanwhile a proposal to link the Causeway Foot and Sowerby services and Illingworth - Rishworth routes was deferred for the time being.

Following the recent closure of the Halifax - Queensbury - Bradford railway line to passenger services, the JOC decided towards the end of 1955 that an inquiry into the need of a replacement bus service via Ovenden and Holmfield should be held following the receipt of a petition signed by 3,065 people. This resulted in a proposal being made by the JOC almost a year later in October 1956 to inaugurate a service from Halifax via Holmfield and Bradshaw to Queensbury where it would connect with the Bradford to Queensbury service operated by Bradford City Transport. After some further delay, the new service eventually commenced operation on 1 April 1957.

Before the new year was a month old, in mid-January 1956 Roderick MacKenzie tendered his resignation as General Manager & Engineer following his appointment as General Manager of Scottish Omnibuses Ltd. at Edinburgh from 1 April. As a result of this announcement, wheels were immediately set in motion to find his replacement and on 6 March Richard Le Fevre, previously General Manager & Engineer of Bury Corporation was selected as successor to the outgoing incumbent and took up his position on 11 June.

Passing along Waterhouse Street, Halifax enroute to Portsmouth in 1973 (no, not in Hampshire but near Todmorden) on route 92, Roe-bodied Daimler CVG6 GJX331 began life in the Corporation fleet in 1956 and was transferred to Halifax JOC in January 1971. Passing to Calderdale Joint Omnibus Committee upon its formation in September 1971, it was renumbered 384 a year later and remained in service until the autumn of 1973 and after a long and illustrious career it was transferred to West Yorkshire PTE in April 1974 as a withdrawn vehicle. *J.Fozard*

Around 1957, Joint Omnibus Committee Park Royal-bodied AEC Regent III 281 (BCP675) was painted in an experimental livery with orange upper and green lower panels separated by a cream band above its lower deck windows. Seen in this form at Pavement Lane, Illingworth enroute to Hubberton on the cross-town 63 service, it was soon repainted back into standard colours, its experimental application being short lived. *R.F.Mack*

On 18 April the Passenger Transport Committee decided against having any further interest in the land between Gt.Albion Street and North Parade for possible use as an extension of the Crossfield bus station and the need for a second bus station on the south side of the town centre after agreeing that the waiting of buses in the town centre could be dispensed with by the operation of through services. A couple of months later on 20 June, following deliberation regarding the charges related to the bus station, the Corporation agreed that these should be fixed as follows :

(a) 50% of yearly net expenditure be allocated to users in proportion to the number of departures against total departures.

(b) 50% of yearly net expenditure allocated to users in proportion to the number of stands occupied against the total number of stands in the bus station.

This, however, was not accepted by the outside operators who referred the matter to the Ministry of Transport to decide the actual charge and to this end an inquiry was held in November 1956. Meanwhile, on 17 September curtailment of the Halifax - Blackley service and the extension of the Triangle - Sowerby Bridge - Elland service to Blackley took place with the associated reduction in Triangle journeys whilst two days later proposals were approved for the reduction of services generally, and particularly in the evenings and on Sundays. As the Transport Department was at this time acutely short of staff and was 130 drivers/conductors below the number required, excessive overtime was being worked and brought a warning from the traffic commissioner against the possible illegal nature of the working hours of many of the drivers. Thus the proposal to reduce services would save 21 evening duties and 12 full day Sunday duties.

The only new buses to be received since August 1954 were 5 Roe-bodied Daimler CVG6 double deckers which entered service in the Corporation fleet in October and November 1956. Numbered 15-9 (GJX327-31), these had teak framed lower decks and alloy top decks and were the last new rear entrance buses to be purchased. With Roderick MacKenzie having now departed and before his successor took up his duties, a start was made on the repainting of the forty or so buses in the revised livery back into the old standard colours and as neither the then chief of the engineering function or the paint shop foreman were impressed with the MacKenzie scheme, the repainting programme was completed in an extremely short space of time!

In the final month of what had proved to be a difficult year, the Town Council at its meeting on 5 December was warned of the need to consider a substantial increase in fares as a result of the massive increase in oil prices because of the Suez crisis. The total extra costs for the undertaking, taking this into account, were envisaged to be in the order of £60,000 over an 18-month period. Prior to any increases being implemented, however, on 17 December timetable revisions affecting 29 Corporation and JOC services brought about by staff shortages and the Suez situation were brought into operation and additionally the Beechwood Road service was withdrawn completely in the evenings. A further consequence of the Suez crisis was the introduction of a 'colene' mixture which was actually a coal distillate that was used with

derv as a 33% mixture and so gave a price advantage of around 2d per gallon at a time when the undertaking was paying around 3/2d per gallon for diesel as well as a saving on the oil-based fuel. The use of this fuel mixture, however, produced a peculiar smell that was noticeable when as a stranger one travelled on a Halifax bus. Not being appreciated by Gardner engines with their low compression ratios, however, led to this form of fuel being quietly phased out in the mid-'sixties when conventional diesel again reigned supreme.

The first significant event in this period related to the purchase of new buses. At its meeting in February 1957 the Passenger Transport Committee opted for the supply of 40 double deckers for the period 1958-62 for 'A' services to be paid for out of a reserve fund which was to be set up rather than by the previous method of borrowing money.

After receiving notification from Huddersfield Corporation that it was to increase the cost of departures from its Upperhead Row bus station in the town from 2d to 3 1/2d, the JOC made a strong protest against this and additionally appealed to the Ministry of Transport. Ironically, Halifax Town Council also protested strongly to the Ministry after an appeal by the private operators using the Crossfield bus station resulted in the charge for departures being fixed at 2p on stage carriage journeys which, it stated, would result in a serious deficit in the operation of the bus station. Following its appeal against the Huddersfield proposal, the Ministry of Transport in November 1958 ruled that there was no case for increasing the charges for the use of Upperhead bus station and that these should remain at 2d. In the mean time, the proposals for a trial period of three months for the previously deferred circular and through services including Wheatley, Illingworth - Rishworth, Causeway Foot - Sowerby and Beechwood Road - Stainland were approved by the Town Council whilst the Ovenden circular services were to be discontinued and the Ovenden Way, Nursery Lane Top and Beechwood Road services coupled with the Stainland/Outlane service to meet basic demand. These changes would, it was said, achieve a saving of 6 buses for the whole of the undertaking and would ease staff shortages, although they would produce an increase in annual mileage of 30,000 miles. Additionally, it was proposed to use part of the car park in Broad Street for the existing Brighouse - Hebden Bridge service and the through running of other services to avoid the necessity of them using the bus station. After giving this scheme its consideration, however, it was rejected by the Highways Committee and thus was not brought into play.

Although no new buses were added to either the Corporation or JOC fleets during 1957, at the end of July a lightweight double decker powered by a new supercharged Daimler 8.6 litre engine was tested on the Brighouse - Hebden Bridge route where it proved more economical on fuel consumption. Additionally a start was made on increasing the seating capacity of all the Corporation and JOC's existing post-war double deckers by fitting most with an extra 3 seats to their upper deck to raise their total capacity from 56 to 59. This took over twelve months to complete with the final examples being thus modified towards the end of 1958. At around this same time the Corporation's 12 heavy Roe-bodied Daimler CVG6s of 1954 vintage had their 112hp Gardner 6LW engines replaced by more powerful 125hp Leyland 0.600 engines while in the late summer of 1957 one of the Metro Cammell-bodied Daimler CVGs's was given a new experimental livery. This employed green lower panels and an orange upper deck - a complete reversal of the established scheme - but following a deluge of letters by Halifax residents to the local press, it quickly returned to the paint shop from where it emerged a few days later back in its 'normal' colours.

Finally, because of the continuing man power shortage, on 17 September the Passenger Transport Committee approved in principle the introduction of one-man-operation on Corporation

The first underfloor-engined single deckers purchased by the Halifax undertakings were delivered to the Corporation in 1958 in the form of Leyland Royal Tiger Worldmasters fitted with Weymann 42-seat bodywork. Illustrating these, 8 (KCP8) climbs Wards End in April 1971 on its way to Newlands.
R.Marshall

services and two months later applied for permission to cut frequencies on 10 Corporation and 10 JOC services. Fortunately, as a result of improvements in staff recruitment, the latter was able to be withdrawn before the cuts could be implemented.

Some of the previous plans which had failed to gain approval were again placed before the Town Council and on this occasion were granted. This allowed a number of through services to commence on 3 March 1958 although through ticketing was not introduced due to the services being operated by the two different authorities, each with its own fares structure, which made accounting difficult. At this same time the renumbered services dispensed with the route number letter suffixes which had been in existence since before the war and the existing Pellon - Illingworth service was replaced by two Mixenden circular routes via Wheatley and Illingworth and Wheatley and Pellon with these also in reverse.

Still keen to evaluate new types of bus, a lowheight AEC Bridgemaster demonstrator was borrowed from its manufacturer for two weeks commencing 13 September and was put to work on the Holywell Green service. Although it performed satisfactorily, it failed to attract the Passenger Transport Committee to place an order for buses of this type and returned from whence it came shortly before the end of the month. This, however, was not the

Its revenue-earning days having ended, Joint Omnibus Committee Roe-bodied AEC Regent III 214 (ACP628) was converted into a driver tuition vehicle in January 1959 and renumbered 412. It continued to service in its new role until March 1966 when it was sold to a Leeds dealer. It is seen here performing its training duties on Oldham Road at Ripponden.   *T.Worsnop*

only new type of bus to make its appearance during 1958 for in October a Weymann-bodied Leyland Royal Tiger Worldmaster made its debut in the Corporation fleet. The first of 9 such buses, it was unique to the Halifax fleet in having an underfloor engine, its entrance door adjacent to the driver and two-pedal semi-automatic transmission. Fitted with 42 seats and sporting electrically-operated ticket machines which made them suitable for one-man-operation, all 9 buses (1-9 : KCP1-9) were placed in revenue-earning service on 10 November on the Washer Lane circular and Siddal services and additionally at off-peak times on the Norton Tower routes. As one door opened, however, another one closed and 1958, as well as marking the start of a new era, ended another when the final buses of pre-war manufacture - Corporation 1938 Roe-bodied AEC Regents 20/1 (JX6902/3) and 1939 Roe-bodied Regent 22 (JX7059) - ran their last journeys and the first withdrawals took place of the post-war AEC Regent IIIs and Regal IIIs..

The wind of change was now starting to gather pace and at the start of January 1959 the first buses to be purchased by the JOC for five years took up their duties mainly on the Hebden Bridge to Brighouse and Halifax to Huddersfield routes. Being another 'first' for Halifax, these were 30ft. long Leyland PD3/4s fitted with Metro Cammell 72-seat bodies featuring a forward entrance with power-operated doors. Numbered 201-8 (KCP10-17) these were to set the standard for all future Halifax buses and provided passengers with a higher standard of comfort and warmer travelling conditions. In the meantime, one of the Corporation's all-Leyland PD2/1s (100 : ACP384) which had been withdrawn from service towards the end of the previous year was converted into a permanent driver training bus in January 1959, a duty it performed for the next four and a half years.

On 2 December 1959 the Town Council gave its approval for changes associated with the town centre traffic plan whereby an extensive one-way system was due for implementation, causing the need for much re-routing of bus services and alterations to their terminal points. Under this scheme, the Brighouse to Hebden Bridge service would no longer call at the bus station and its passengers would instead be picked up in Silver Street whilst similarly the Illingworth/Causeway Foot - Rishworth/Sowerby buses would use stands in Waterhouse Street rather than in the bus station. Silver Street was also to be the terminal for the Highroad Well route in place of George Square and the West End via Pellon Lane service was to collect its passengers at Fountain Street rather than Commercial Street. Due to the new one-way streets the services to Wainstalls, Mixenden and Norton Tower were re-routed to operate via Gt.Albion Street, St.James Road and St.James Street to Pellon Lane while the Cousin Lane, Wheatley, Illingworth and Mixenden stands were moved to the opposite side of Crossley Street. All these changes were implemented on 8 February 1960 when the new traffic scheme was brought into operation on an experimental basis before becoming permanent in July.

The first year of the new decade witnessed the arrival of a large number of new buses which were divided equally between the Corporation and JOC fleets. The first 18 were 30ft.long AEC Regent Vs fitted with forward entrance Metro Cammell 72-seat bodywork. Taking up their duties between January and March,

The last three pre-war AEC Regents to operate in Halifax, Corporation Roe-bodied 20, 21 & 22 (JX6902/3 & JX7059) are posed for the photographer before leaving Skircoat Road depot on their final day in service in 1958.
R.Marshall collection

11-8 (LJX11-8) were allocated to the Corporation with 211-8 (LJX211-8) being for the JOC. Later in the year in November, these were joined by 16 Leyland PD2/37s which had 64-seat forward entrance Metro Cammell bodywork with 21-8 (MJX21-8)

being for the Corporation and 221-8 (MCP221-8) for the JOC. Of these buses, no.27 was exhibited at the Commercial Motor Show at London's Earls Court in October prior to its delivery to Halifax.

Apart from the changes associated with the town's new traffic

The first forward entrance double deckers to be purchased by the Halifax undertaking were MCCW-bodied Leyland PD3/4s in 1959 which were allocated to the Joint Omnibus Committee fleet. One of these buses, 206 (KCP15) is seen leaving Crossfield bus station on a journey to Brighouse on the through service from Hebden Bridge. *T.Worsnop*

Stopping outside Smith Bulmers on Holdsworth Road, Holmfield on its way to Halifax in August 1966 is Joint Omnibus Committee MCCW-bodied AEC Regent V 211 (LJX211) which was then six years old.
R.Marshall

scheme and a few minor route and stand changes in April and
July, 1960 proved to be a comparatively quiet year for the
Transport Department with the only other development worthy of
note being that which took place on 17 December when early
morning staff buses became available to the general public at a
flat fare of 6d.

Stability continued throughout 1961 with the established
pattern of services remaining largely unchanged except for some
minor re-routing, the extension on 7 August of the Brighouse -
Field Lane service to Burnsall Road, Bedale Avenue and Highfield
Road and the withdrawal on 18 September of the through Halifax
- Southowram - Brighouse route.

Only one new bus was received during the year, this being an
experimental standee-type single decker with seating for 33
passengers and standing capacity for a further 26. Based on an
underfloor-engined Leyland Leopard chassis, its Weymann body
had a front entrance and centre exit, making it eminently suitable
for one-man-operation and allowing speedy boarding and
alighting. Allocated to the JOC fleet and numbered 231
(OCP231), it made its debut at the start of August and was used
on a variety of routes. Despite its innovative nature, however, this
bus never proved popular with passengers or drivers. Meanwhile,
in an attempt to improve the power output of the Corporation's
1954 Roe-bodied Daimler CVG6s, no.93 was experimentally fitted
with a supercharged Daimler engine in April.

1962 began with the opening in January of another new
school, Holy Trinity, at the schoolbase at Illingworth where other
educational establishments were already located. This led to the
need for an additional bus to be added to the Corporation fleet in
order to be able to maintain the increased service of school
specials and as well as staggering school hours to accommodate
these extra needs, the Halifax terminal of all the buses operating
to the schoolbase was standardised at Gt.Albion Street.

Unlike the previous year, a large quantity of new buses were
taken into stock during 1962, all of which took up their duties from
July onwards. The first to appear were 9 Leyland Leopard single
deckers for the Corporation (31-9 : PJX31-9) and 7 for the JOC
(232-8 : PJX232-8). Fitted with front entrance 42-seat Weymann
bodies, these were used to replace a substantial number of the
1949 AEC Regal IIIs in addition to enabling the Halifax -
Southowram - Brighouse service to be restored to its former route
and frequency from 13 August. Later, in November and
December the Leopards were joined by 16 forward entrance
Weymann-bodied Leyland PD2/37 double deckers which were
divided equally between the two fleets with the Corporation
receiving 41-8 (PJX41-8) and the JOC 241-8 (PJX241-8). Prior to
their arrival, one of the JOC's 1959 Leyland PD3/4s (206) was
loaned to Oldham Corporation in July for evaluation by that
municipal undertaking.

As an experiment, from 17 December certain inward off-peak
journeys on the Heptonstall route were diverted through the
Willowfield Estate between Burnley Road and Rochdale Road
although this proved to be unsuccessful and the service was
reinstated to its earlier form on 20 May 1963. Prior to this, more
Corporation services including Northowram, Copley and Shibden
were converted to one-man-operation on 11 March 1963 at the
same time that alternate journeys, withdrawn since the re-linking
of services, to Mixenden via Wheatley reverted to operating via
City Lane.

A few months before the General Manager & Engineer
Richard Le Fevre came to retire on 8 October 1963, following
trials with a Maidstone & District bus of this type, he introduced a
brand new make of bus to Halifax in the shape of the Albion
Nimbus of which 10 (250-9 : RJX250-9) made their debut in the
JOC fleet in May and June. Fitted with Weymann 31-seat
bodywork, these small underfloor-engined buses had been
designed for use on rural routes and there was a proposal to use
them as feeder vehicles to connect such places as Cragg Vale
and Heptonstall with the main Calder Valley bus route although
transfer ticket difficulties and the fact that passengers would not
appreciate having to change buses led to the retention of most of
the through routes. It quickly became apparent that lightweight
buses and the gradients around Halifax were not compatible and
within a year 5 of the 10 buses had required an engine change
with the condition of a further 3 being suspect. Indeed, such was
the catalogue of defects related to these buses that their
availability was only around 60% and as a consequence their
lives in Halifax were to prove brief with their withdrawal
commencing in 1965 and being completed two years later.

Enroute to West End, Weymann-bodied Leyland Worldmaster 373 (KCP3) travels along Free School Lane, Savile Park in summer sunshine. New to the Corporation in 1958, it was transferred to the Joint Omnibus Committee in June 1972. *N.Harris*

Approaching North Bridge from Crosshill on its way to Cousin Lane is Corporation Park Royal-bodied AEC Regent III 77 (CCP609). *N.Harris*

Joint Omnibus Committee Weymann-bodied Albion Nimbus 354 (RJX254) rests in Bull Close Lane, Halifax after completing a private hire duty. *N.Harris*

Seen in semi-rural surroundings at Causewayfoot in the mid 'sixties, Joint Omnibus Committee MCCW-bodied Daimler CVG6 299 (DCP852) was bound for Wainstalls on route 21. *N.Harris*

Travelling along Waterhouse Street, Halifax in August 1969, Weymann-bodied Leyland PD2/37 44 (PJX44) is followed by MCCW-bodied AEC Regent V 15 (LJX15), both of which were members of the Corporation fleet. *R.Marshall*

Leaving Crossfield bus station, Halifax at the start of its journey to Brighouse whilst on loan to Halifax Corporation for evaluation is Maidstone & District Weymann-bodied Albion Nimbus 143SMG. *K.A.Jenkinson collection*

Previous page :

Top left : **Heading along Huddersfield Road, Halifax is forward entrance MCCW-bodied AEC Regent V 17 (LJX17) which was new to the Corporation in March 1960.** *N.Harris*

Top right : **Climbing Cain Lane, Southowram on its return journey to Halifax on route 50 is Joint Omnibus Committee Pennine-bodied AEC Reliance 251 (ECP951D)** *N.Harris*

Centre left upper : **One of a pair of Metro Scania buses borrowed for evaluation in December 1970, VWD452H is seen at Higgin Lane, Southowram whilst operating the Brighouse to Heptonstall service.** *N.Harris*

Centre right : **One of the vehicles inherited by the Joint Omnibus Committee from Hebble Motor Services in March 1971, Burlingham-bodied Leyland Leopard 306 (5876W) is seen here at Southowram whilst operating route 50.** *N.Harris*

Centre left lower : **Passing the old Crossley's carpet factory at Dean Clough enroute to Wainstalls whilst undergoing evaluation in 1969 is Seddon RU demonstrator TBU598G.** *N.Harris*

Bottom left : **Joint Omnibus Committee Weymann-bodied Leyland PD2/37 246 (PJX246) collects its Halifax-bound passengers at Sowerby Bridge.** *N.Harris*

Bottom right : **Standing at Rishworth terminus awaiting its departure to Illingworth in May 1964 whilst being tested in service by the Halifax undertaking is London Transport's unique front entrance Routemaster 254CLT.** *N.Harris*

As a consequence of the arrival of the Albions, the JOC converted a number of its services to one-man-operation in September, these being Brighouse - Field Lane; Brighouse - Southowram and Mill Bank (except at peak times) and Elland - Ripponden, the latter of which was already operated on a 50% one-man basis.

Returning to the fleet, the Corporation lost two of its buses due to accident damage during 1963, the first being Park Royal-bodied AEC Regent III no.59 (ACP902) in February, the second all-Leyland PD2/1 107 (ACP391) on 14 June when it struck a low bridge at West Vale. After remaining in store for several years, no.59 was dismantled at Skircoat Road depot by a scrap dealer in May 1969 whilst no.107 was converted to open-top format and put to use as a driver training bus and snow plough, replacing the former driver training Leyland PD2/1 (100) in the process. Having been unsuccessful, the JOC's experimental dual-door Leyland Leopard (231) was returned to Weymann's factory at Addlestone during the latter part of 1962 for rebuilding to standard front entrance layout and in its new form as a 42-seater it returned to Halifax in January 1963.

Following the retirement of Richard Le Fevre, Geoffrey G. Hilditch returned from Great Yarmouth Corporation where he had been General Manager & Engineer to Halifax take over as the undertaking's General Manager & Engineer with effect from 5 November. Soon after his arrival, 8 new buses were delivered to the Corporation in the form of forward entrance Weymann-bodied Leyland PD3/4s numbered 51-8 (TCP51-8). Of these, 3 were placed in service in December with the remaining 5 taking up their duties in January 1964.

Illustrating the type of route for which they were purchased, 254 (RJX254), one of the Joint Omnibus Committee's Weymann-bodied Albion Nimbuses, squeezes its way through a narrow section of route 53 to Cragg Vale. *K.A.Jenkinson collection*

TESTING TIMES

Following G.G.Hilditch's arrival back in Halifax, a massive evaluation programme was put into place in order to compare different types of buses prior to placing new orders. First to arrive in the town was 7552MX, a Park Royal-bodied AEC Renown demonstrator which made its debut on 7 April and stayed until 10 May whilst following it on 9 April was 565CRW, an Alexander-bodied Daimler Fleetline which was evaluated for three weeks. Adding to the scene was Strachan-bodied Guy Arab IV 888DUK which arrived on 24 April and departed four weeks later and London Transport's unique forward entrance AEC Routemaster 254CLT which was used on various services from 27 April to 10 May. Before all of the above had returned from whence they came, an Alexander-bodied Leyland Atlantean demonstrator (SGD669) arrived in the town on 20 May, this giving the false impression that it had been purchased by the undertaking in view of it being painted in the livery of its original owner Glasgow Corporation, whose orange, green & cream colours were similar to those of Halifax. Following the Atlantean's departure on 9 June, it was three months before the next stranger to Halifax was to be seen, this time a Metro Cammell-bodied Leyland Atlantean borrowed not from its manufacturer, but from Wallasey Corporation on 21 September. In exchange, one of the Corporation's Weymann-bodied Leyland PD3/4s (52) was loaned to the Wirral undertaking, with both buses returning to their respective owners on 12 October. The last of the buses borrowed for in-service tests was an NCME-bodied Dennis Loline demonstrator which arrived on 13 November and departed on 7 December and like all the others earlier in the year, it too was used on a variety of services in order to be able to evaluate its performance and economy.

In addition to the wide variety of buses that had been seen, albeit temporarily, on the streets of Halifax during 1964, some more strangers appeared in July on a slightly more permanent basis. Due to the late delivery of new buses caused by a strike at Weymann's factory, it had been found necessary to transfer the order to Chas.H.Roe at Leeds and to cover for the delay resulting from this, 4 Roe-bodied AEC Regent IIIs were purchased from W.Norths (dealers) in July. Dating from 1947, these had

Travelling along Burnley Road at Mytholmroyd on its way from Brighouse to Hebden Bridge is forward entrance Strachan-bodied Guy Arab IV demonstrator 888DUK which was borrowed by Halifax Corporation for four weeks in April/May 1964.   *R.F.Mack*

Travelling along Burnley Road, King Cross on its way from Hebden Bridge to Brighouse whilst on loan to Halifax for evaluation in November 1964 is NCME-bodied Dennis Loline demonstrator EPG179B.   *R.F.Mack*

One of five ex.Leeds City Transport Roe-bodied AEC Regent IIIs purchased in 1964, 440 was initially allocated to the Corporation fleet (in which it was numbered 40) but was transferred to the JOC in September 1965, a few weeks before its withdrawal from service. Seen here at the bus park close to Crossfield bus station in October 1965, it still wore the dark green livery of its former owner.
R.F.Mack

Acquired by the Joint Omnibus Committee Timpson of London in 1966, Park Royal-bodied AEC Reliance coach 261 (NRK350) rests in the yard of West Riding's Belle Isle depot at Wakefield. *N.Harris*

Inherited by the Joint Omnibus Committee from Hebble Motor Services in February 1971, Weymann-bodied AEC Regent V 312 (AJX410B) picks up its passengers in Dudwell Lane before continuing its journey to Bradford. *N.Harris*

One of four buses acquired by Calderdale Joint Omnibus Committee from Maidstone & District in 1972 to cover a temporary vehicle shortage, highbridge Park Royal-bodied AEC Regent V 362 (VKR479) seen here in King Edward Street retained the livery of its previous owned for the duration of its brief life in Halifax.
N.Harris

Halifax's standard rear engined double decker was the NCME-bodied Daimler Fleetline, an example of which (Joint Omnibus Committee 290 - JJX597G) is seen at Crossfield bus station, Halifax awaiting its departure to Queensbury. *N.Harris*

One of a trio of dual-purpose Plaxton-bodied Seddon RUs bought by the Joint Omnibus Committee in 1970, 317 (MJX17J) climbs out of Halifax on a journey to Leeds on route 8.   *N.Harris*

New to Hebble but acquired by the Joint Omnibus Committee from Yorkshire Woollen District Transport in August 1971, NCME-bodied Daimler Fleetline 294 (DJX351D) was looking worse for wear as it collected its passengers at Queensbury enroute from Bradford to Halifax.   *N.Harris*

One of a pair of Park Royal-bodied AEC Monocoaches purchased by the Corporation from Sheffield JOC in 1965, 19 (TWJ505) is seen here at Brighouse bus station.   *N.Harris*

Corporation Willowbrook-bodied Daimler Fleetline 108 (FJX508E) with its 'pay as you enter' sign uncovered stands in Powell Street, Halifax prior to its departure on route 4 to Siddal.   *N.Harris*

previously been operated by Leeds City Transport and still wore that undertaking's two-tone green livery. Not being intended to remain in the fleet for long, they were all placed in service by their new owner without being repainted, with 1 being allocated to the Corporation and the remaining 3 to the JOC. Later, in November a fifth bus of this type was obtained from the same source (and was again ex.Leeds City Transport) for the Corporation fleet while 2 new dual-purpose seated Willowbrook-bodied Leyland Leopards for the JOC arrived in October, the latter being purchased for the purpose of attracting additional private hire work. Meanwhile, following the experimental fitting of Corporation Daimler CVG6 93 with a supercharged Daimler engine in 1961, sister bus 94 was given a more powerful Gardner 6LX engine in April 1964. Perhaps the most unusual occurrence within the fleet, however, was the transfer of one of the JOC's 1949 AEC Regal III single deckers to the Corporation in October and its return to the JOC a month later. On each occasion it was renumbered, being originally 269, 99 when it joined the Corporation fleet, and 268 when it resumed its duties with the JOC!

Following the curtailing of the Elland - Triangle service at Sowerby Bridge during off-peak times and its combination with

Approaching Holywell Green terminus whilst on loan to Halifax Corporation for evaluation in 1958 is Park Royal-bodied AEC Bridgemaster demonstrator 76MME.
K.A.Jenkinson collection

New to the Joint Omnibus Committee in 1964, dual purpose Willowbrook-bodied Leyland leopard 270 (AJX270B) is seen here in James Street, Elland.
T.Worsnop collection

the Blackley service to enable one-man-operation from 3 February 1964, the Queens Road service was also converted to OMO on Sundays only from 15 March. Some weeks later on 27 April, the Brighouse - Field Lane Estate route was extended from Highfield Road to Nunnery Lane and during the penultimate month of the year a new service was inaugurated on 16 November from Brighouse bus station to Oaklands Estate.

After an extremely eventful year, it was wondered how 1965 would compare and within a few weeks the almost sanctimonious refusal to allow adverts, as a source of revenue, on Halifax buses was reversed at a meeting of the Town Council in February when it was agreed to permit adverts to be carried on the side and lower rear panels of buses, subject to the adherence of strictly enforced standards. Following this, a major reshuffle of services was undertaken on 26 April when in addition, fare stage distances were reduced from a 1/2 to 1/3 of a mile which meant, in effect, that most fares would increase by 1d or 2d, with the minimum 3d fare being retained, and by some miracle it was found possible to hold the new scales until 1969! The main service revisions were as follows :

(a) The Beech Road - Claremount service ceased to be a through route and became Beech Road - Rye Lane (1) with no through fares.

(b) The General Hospital -West End services (31/32) were completely withdrawn. The Copley service was extended to West End via Hopwood Lane to become 31 while the 32 service had only a peak-hours operation between George Street and West End via King Cross. The Northowram services were extended to the General Hospital, this latter section becoming OMO.

(c) The Highroad Well service was linked to the Ovenden - Mixenden/Wheatley - Mixenden/Mount Tabor - Mixenden services with through fares and alternate journeys operating via Hebble Lane rather than the steep City Lane.

(d) The Outlane/Stainland - Ovenden services were split, with the Halifax - Beechwood Road service becoming 18 and returning via Shay Lane. The 17 ran in the opposite direction while the Outlane service via Stainland Road was numbered 38 with Stainland short workings becoming 39. Service 57 to Holywell Green was extended to Outlane to become 37.

(e) Also split were the Rishworth - Illingworth (62) and Sowerby - Causeway Foot (63) services, the Illingworth route becoming 20 and the Causeway Foot service being linked with Wainstalls (21). All the Sowerby/Rishworth journeys operated to a terminal point in George Street via Bull Green, Fountain Street and Commercial Street.

(f) The Midgley (65), Booth (66) and Beech Road (67) services were transferred to Wards End via Trinity Road and Blackwall.

(g) The Bradshaw/Queensbury service (27) operated via Keighley Road and Pavement Lane, joining its former route at Bradshaw post office while the 9 to Cousin Lane operated on its return in a loop via Furness Drive, Furness Grove, Turner Avenue South and Bank Edge Road. This latter diversion lasted only until November 1967, however, when the service reverted to its former route.

(h) The termini of the Shibden (33) and Brighouse via Southowram (50) services were transferred from the bus station to Westgate and Albion Street respectively.

Later, on 1 July, a concessionary fare scheme was introduced which allowed half-price travel between 9.30am and 12noon and 2.00pm and 4.00pm (weekdays only) on Corporation services to people over 70 years of age upon production of a pass costing 2/6d. The JOC, however, could not accept these passes on its services unless authorised by the British Railways Board who in the event were unwilling to grant this. Also in July the Northowram service to the Borough boundary was extended to the Yew Tree Inn following the expiry of the lease for turning purposes at the

The first of a number of secondhand coaches to be purchased by the Joint Omnibus Committee was acquired in March 1965 in the form of a Park Royal-bodied AEC Reliance which had begun life with Bourne & Balmer of Croydon in 1954. Given fleet number 200, MBY347 is seen here at Thirsk Market Place whilst undertaking a private hire duty. In 1967 it was fitted with a new Plaxton Panorama coach body and survived in the fleet long enough to be taken over by West Yorkshire PTE in April 1974. *J.Fozard*

New in 1965, Joint Omnibus Committee 288 (CJX328C), a Weymann-bodied Leyland PD2/37, prepares to leave its stand in Crossfield bus station, Halifax at the start of its hilly journey to Queensbury on route 40.
K.A.Jenkinson collection

Standing on the forecourt of Skircoat Road depot is Corporation forward entrance Roe-bodied Leyland PD2/37 65 (CCP65C) which was new in 1965. *T.Worsnop*

Queen Victoria Inn. The new concessionary scheme relating to the Corporation services was later modified on 6 January 1966 to operate through from 9.30am to 4.00pm without the lunchtime break and a month afterwards on 7 February the age limit was reduced to 65 and over for men and 60 and over for women to bring it in line with their pensionable ages.

The fleet was meanwhile enhanced with the purchase by the JOC in March 1965 from W.Norths (dealers) of Sherburn-in-Elmet of an accident-damaged centre entrance 41-seat Park Royal-bodied AEC Reliance coach (200 : MBY347) which had begun life in 1954 with Bourne & Balmer Ltd. of Croydon. This was acquired initially to provide another set of seats in order to be able to convert a further Albion Nimbus to dual-purpose status, but after finding the damage to be much lighter than had been seemed at first sight, it was instead repaired in the Skircoat Road workshops as an addition to the private hire fleet and took up its new duties in July painted in a predominantly cream livery with green and orange relief. Also purchased from W.Norths in May 1965 for the Corporation fleet were two secondhand 44-seat Park Royal-bodied AEC Monocoaches (19/20 : TWJ505/6) which dated from 1955 and originated with Sheffield Joint Omnibus Committee. These were joined in September and October by 8 new Roe-bodied Leyland PD2/37s (59-66 : CCP159-66C) for the Corporation fleet and between September and December new Roe-bodied Leyland PD2/37s 278/9 (CCP523/4C), Weymann-bodied Leyland PD2/37s 280-9 (CJX320-9C) and dual-purpose seated Willowbrook-bodied Leyland Leopard 267 (CJX275C) for the JOC. In addition, a 1949 all-Leyland PD2/1, Park Royal-bodied AEC Regent III and one of the ex.Leeds City Transport Roe-bodied AEC Regent IIIs (still in its former owner's livery!) were transferred from the Corporation to the JOC in September. As it transpired, the latter three buses were to spend only a few months with their new owner with the PD2/1 and Leeds Regent together with the Corporation's four ex.Leeds buses all being withdrawn before the end of the year and the Park Royal-bodied Regent III surviving only into the early months of 1966. Surprisingly, also reappearing in September for three weeks was 565CRW, the Alexander-bodied Daimler Fleetline demonstrator which had previously been borrowed in 1964.

1966 began with plans being laid to build a new bus-washing plant at the rear of Skircoat Road depot which, in addition to updating this facility would also release the site of the old bus-wash for use as a new office block. In May, Skircoat Road's workshops, finding themselves with some spare capacity began to undertake repair work on vehicles owned by Todmorden Joint Omnibus Committee.

Early in the new year further service changes were undertaken, albeit of a minor nature, and amongst these was the re-siting of the terminus (on safety grounds) of the Beech Road service to Dearden Street, off Tuel Lane to eliminate the reversing that had previously been necessary and the moving at Easter of the Heptonstall terminus from the 'rat hole' in Towngate to a point 1,047 yards distant through the narrow winding village street to form a loop in a housing estate. Additionally, the reversing point at Mytholm was moved from Church Lane to the West Riding County Council depot in Burnley Road while on 25 July the Tuel

Lane - Boulderclough service was converted to one-man-operation. Prior to this, an additional Countryside Tour was inaugurated on 30 May which included Wheatley, Bradshaw, Queensbury, Brighouse, Rastrick, Nont Sarahs, Barkisland, Norland and West Vale in its itinerary at a fare of 3/- and on its first day of operation it incredibly required 26 vehicles.

Following an amount of research into the undertaking's ticket issuing system, a changeover to TIM machines was approved in principle by the JOC and it was agreed to undertake trials on all routes before converting some to this new system. In the meantime, keen to further expand its private hire facilities the JOC purchased 5 more AEC Reliance coaches which had originated with Bourne & Balmer, 3 of which had Burlingham bodies and the other 2 Park Royal coachwork. Four of these

made their debut in February 1966 with the remaining example following in June and after being repainted into the predominantly cream coach livery of their new owner and numbered 260-4, they took up their duties mainly on the daily (weekday) Meredith & Drew contract which required 6 vehicles to transport workers to and from its Halifax factory from South Yorkshire. Additionally, it was in 1966 that the first sortie overseas was undertaken when one of the JOC's Willowbrook-bodied single deckers ventured as far afield as Switzerland on a private hire duty. Meanwhile, the 8 new Weymann-bodied Leyland PD2/37s (67-74 : DCP67-74D) placed in service in January in the Corporation fleet proved to be the last of this type to be purchased with the buses delivered later in the year marking the start of a new era in being of rear-engine layout. Daimler Fleetlines with NCME 75-seat bodies, the first to

The first rear engined double deckers to be purchased were seven NCME-bodied Daimler Fleetlines which took up their duties in the Corporation fleet in the autumn of 1966. One of these, ECP683D was transferred to the Joint Omnibus Committee in 1971 and is seen in Commercial Street, Halifax after receiving its new fleet number 293. *T.Worsnop collection*

arrive, Corporation 105 (ECP685D) took up its duties on 1 September whilst sister buses 99-104 (ECP679-84D) entered service in October and November. All the new vehicles for the JOC during this year were of single deck configuration and comprised another dual-purpose seated Willowbrook-bodied Leyland Leopard (268 : DJX143D) in April, 2 similarly-bodied AEC Reliances (265/6 : EJX65/6D) in November and 7 Pennine-bodied AEC Reliances (249-55 : ECP949-55D) between October 1966 and February 1967, 249 having first been exhibited at the 1966 Commercial Motor Show at Earls Court, London. Of the latter, although all were delivered fitted with 39 bus seats, 252 was

reseated with the dual-purpose seats removed from a pair of withdrawn Albion Nimbuses before its entry into service. Obtained as replacements for the last of the 31-seat Albions, 249-55 were of 27ft. length and 7ft.6in width so as to be suitable for operation on rural routes and in addition, their arrival allowed the last AEC Regal III to be withdrawn. Once again a couple of demonstrators were borrowed from their manufacturers for evaluation, one of which was a Marshall-bodied single deck Daimler Roadliner (CVC124C) which was used from 15 to 24 August, the other being Alexander-bodied Daimler Fleetline 565CRW from 9 August to 7 September, this being its third visit to Halifax since 1964!

Seen heading to Highroad Well whilst being evaluated by Halifax Corporation in August 1966 is Marshall-bodied Daimler SRC6 demonstrator CVC124C. *K.A.Jenkinson collection*

In 1966 the Joint Omnibus Committee purchased seven short AEC Reliances with Pennine bodywork which featured a short overhang aft of the rear axle. Pictured at Ward End in 1971, 253 (ECP953D) appears to have suffered some accident damage to its lower side panels. *J.Fozard*

Fleetline double deckers 97/8 (GJX317/8F) which took up their duties with the Corporation in September while moving from the Corporation to the JOC in June/July were AEC Monocoaches 19/20 (renumbered 219/20 by the JOC) and 2 of the 1954 Roe-bodied Daimler CVG6s. Following a decision to rebody four of the JOC's ex.Bourne & Balmer AEC Reliance coaches, 256 (MBY347) was despatched to Plaxton at Scarborough for this purpose during the early autumn, returning to Halifax in October 1967 sporting a stylish new Panorama 43-seat body. A month later, 259 (TGJ484) was similarly treated as was 258 (NRK350) in January 1968 and 257 (PXO974) in July 1968. Yet again a number of demonstrators were borrowed and put through their paces on various services with a Strachan-bodied Leyland Panther Cub (YTD771D) being tested from 8 to 12 May, Park Royal-bodied Leyland Atlantean KTD551C from 5 to 16 June and a Duple coach-bodied Daimler Roadliner (CWK641C) for a short

Despite displaying Highroad Well in its destination screen, JOC NCME-bodied Dennis Loline 304 (FCP304E) was on a private hire duty when caught by the camera in 1967.
K.A.Jenkinson

Two of the AEC Reliances purchased from Timpsons of London in 1966 - 259 (TGJ484) and 258 (NRK350) are seen here after being given new Plaxton Panorama bodies in 1968.
T.Worsnop collection

1967 dawned and brought two more new types of bus into the Halifax fleets in addition to further Daimler Fleetlines with both the Corporation and JOC benefiting from their arrival. Of the new types, 3 were single deck rear-engined Daimler Fleetlines for the Corporation (106-8 (FJX506-8E), both of which were fitted with 45-seat Willowbrook bus bodies and were placed in service in June while for the JOC came 5 NCME-bodied Dennis Lolines (300-4 : FCP300-4E). These were first used on Countryside Tour no.4 which commenced on 27 March taking in West Vale, Greetland, Krumlin, Dean Head (site of the construction of the M62 motorway and adjacent Scammonden Dam), Pole Moor, Nont Sarahs, Outlane and Brighouse as well as being frequently employed on the lucrative Meredith & Drew contracts. Completing the year's new vehicle intake were NCME-bodied Daimler

period in September. In the event, however, none of these attracted orders from the Halifax undertaking.

Although the service network remained comparatively stable throughout 1967, after fifteen years of campaigning a service between Elland and Exley was finally started on 18 September operating two journeys in each direction on Mondays, Wednesdays and Fridays only, although due to a lack of patronage from 1 April 1968 it was reduced to Wednesday only operation. On 27 November the Shibden service was extended to Queensbury (Granby Street) via Green Lane, Syke lane, Jackson Hill and Hungerhill Estate and was at that same time transferred from the Corporation to the JOC with a protected fare being applied in favour of the more direct Hebble Motor Services Halifax - Queensbury - Bradford service. Somewhat surprisingly, this

Amongst the buses borrowed for evaluation during the 'sixties was Park Royal-bodied Leyland Atlantean demonstrator KTD551C which is seen in June 1967 turning at Queensbury Cenotaph in preparation for its return journey to Halifax. In the background is Bradford City Transport Weymann-bodied AEC Regent III 4 (FKY4) which was working its owner's Queensbury - Bradford service.
N.Harris

Leyland PD2/1 ACP391 was converted into a replica of one of Halifax's original open-top trams for the celebrations to mark the 70th anniversary of municipal transport in the town.
K.A.Jenkinson collection

service reverted back to Corporation control on 1 January 1968 in order to qualify for the concessionary fares facility.

After a quiet start, 1968 brought with it a major inter-urban development when in 1 April two new services were launched between Halifax and Sheffield numbered 68 and X68, each alternating with the other on an hourly frequency and maintained jointly by Sheffield JOC, Huddersfield JOC, Halifax JOC and Yorkshire Traction. Whilst the X68 ran on an express basis, the 68 operated via Chapeltown and replaced the previous Huddersfield - Sheffield service. The commencement of this operation resulted in the pooling of mileage on the Halifax - Huddersfield service in the proportion of 25% to Huddersfield and 75% to Halifax as a means of sharing any loss of revenue on the same route between the two towns caused by the introduction of the Sheffield services. On Saturdays and Sundays, however, the new service was operated only by Yorkshire Traction and Sheffield JOC whilst also from 1 April the Huddersfield terminus of the service from Halifax was moved to the bottom of New North Road due to the closure of Upperhead Row bus station for

Acquired for use as a driver tuition vehicle in November 1968, former East Yorkshire Motor Services Roe-bodied Leyland PD2/12 403 (MKH81) is seen here at Bradshaw terminus. Its unusually shaped roof was necessary to allow it passage through the North Bar at Beverley and was common to most East Yorkshire double deckers.
R.F.Mack

redevelopment with the Halifax terminus moving from Alexandra Street to Crossfield bus station on 29 July. On this same day, one-man-operation was carried a stage further when the Beechwood Road circular was thus converted and linked to the Queens Road service while major revisions were undertaken in the Ovenden and Illingworth areas. Finally, on 9 October dispensation was given from the following Easter to the extension by six miles of Countryside Tour No.4 to Delph to provide better refreshment facilities and also to the diversion of the Midgley and Booth services at Luddenden to operate via Kershaw Estate.

Another milestone was marked in the history of municipal transport in Halifax when on 15 June its 70th anniversary was celebrated as part of the Halifax Charity Gala with a parade of around 30 preserved buses from Skircoat Road depot to Manor Heath where they were put on display. For this occasion, in addition to borrowing various vintage buses from the Science Museum collection in London, the undertaking's driver training/tree lopper Leyland PD2/1 107 (ACP391) was converted into a replica 1898 Halifax tram whilst on the previous day (14 June) the new office block at Skircoat Road depot was officially opened.

Fleet changes during 1968 saw more new buses join both the Corporation and JOC fleets as well as several inter-fleet transfers and the arrival of further secondhand vehicles and additionally marked the passing of the last of the once numerous AEC Regent IIIs, the final example of which (277 : BCP671) was purchased from the JOC in May 1969 by a local preservationist and of which more later. Of the new buses, the Corporation received another

Willowbrook-bodied single deck Daimler Fleetline together with 2 more NCME-bodied double deck examples of this type (95/6 : JJX595/6G) in October, the single decker (111 : JJX371G) having been exhibited at the Commercial Motor Show prior to delivery to Halifax. Only a few weeks after its entry into service, 111 was sent on loan to Sheffield Corporation on 13 November in exchange for one of that undertaking's dual-door Atlanteans (WWB193G) which was evaluated in Halifax for two weeks with both buses being returned to their rightful owners on the penultimate day of that month. For the JOC came a trio of dual-purpose seated Willowbrook-bodied AEC Reliances (262-4 : JCP322-4F) which were placed in service on 1 August and 2 NCME-bodied Daimler Fleetline double deckers (290/1 : JJX597/8G) in October. Additionally, the JOC further strengthened its coach fleet with the purchase in March from Hughes (dealer), Gomersal of a fourteen year-old Burlingham-bodied AEC Reliance (200 : ODK770) which had started life with Yelloway of Rochdale while the Corporation surprisingly bought a 1952 Leyland PD2/12 from W.Norths (dealer) in November for dedicated use as a driver training bus. New to East Yorkshire Motor Services, this full-fronted Roe-bodied double decker was unusual in featuring a specially contoured roof to allow it passage beneath the North Bar at Beverley and in some ways brought back memories of Halifax's early AEC Regents which also had unusually shaped roofs. Completing the changes of 1968 as far as the fleet was concerned was the transfer of 2 Roe-bodied Daimler CVG6s from the Corporation to the JOC in July in exchange for 2 MCCW-bodied Daimler CVG6s, the latter being required by the Corporation due to a weight restriction applied to North Bridge while it was being strengthened.

EXPANDED INTO A NEW JOINT OMNIBUS COMMITTEE

Halifax's close association with the railways which had lasted almost forty years came to an end on 1 January 1969 when the former British Railways Board part of the assets and liabilities of the Joint Omnibus Committee were vested, under the Transport Act 1968, in Amalgamated Passenger Transport Ltd. a subsidiary of the newly-created National Bus Company. From its base at the Yorkshire Woollen District Transport headquarters at Saville Town, Dewsbury, APT provided a new panel of nominees who took over from the former BRB representatives attending their last JOC meeting on 19 January. Almost before the new regime had settled in, during May the Corporation's Transport and Passenger Transport Committees were merged and placed under the wing of the Transport and Cleansing Committee.

Meanwhile, the updating of both the Corporation and JOC fleets continued and in February 1969 the former received 2 new Pennine-bodied Daimler Fleetline single deckers (109/10 : KCP379/80G) which were followed two months later by 3 similar buses fitted with Willowbrook bodies (112-4 : KCP422-4G). All the 5 new single deckers for the JOC were AEC Reliances with Plaxton bodywork and of these 273-5 (KCP873-5G) were 43-seat coaches which entered service in April while 276/7 (KCP876/7G) had 43 dual-purpose type seats and made their debut in June. It was on 10 June, however, that the surprise of the year took place when the JOC's 9 month-old NCME-bodied Daimler Fleetline 291 was sold to Transport Vehicles (Daimler) Ltd. for use as an overseas demonstrator. Still wearing its Halifax livery of orange, green and cream, it was shipped to Cape Town City Transport in South Africa in October 1969 and was later sold to that undertaking. In its place Transport Vehicles provided Halifax JOC with a new identical bus in February 1970, this taking the fleet number (291) of the vehicle it replaced.

Yet again, the Corporation and JOC's service network remained stable throughout the year with the only changes of note taking place on 25 August 1969 when the Rye Lane - Claremount route being split to allow double deckers to continue to be used on the Rye Lane section whilst the Claremount service was converted to OMO using single deckers. Additionally, on this same date the Halifax - Midgley (65), Halifax - Booth (66) and Halifax - Tuel Lane (67) services were also converted to OMO.

New legislation in March 1969 (Transport Act 1968) enabled local authorities to subsidise travel concessions on non-local authority-owned buses through contributions from the rates, and as a result, from 1 January 1970 concessionary fares for senior citizens were extended to JOC services but applied only to journeys taken wholly within the County Borough of Halifax boundary. At the same time, Sowerby Bridge UDC was also one of the first local authorities to introduce concessionary travel on buses by the purchase of 80 x 3d tickets for use by each pensioner for payment of fares on JOC services. Soon after the above took place, on 15 March 1970 new regulations came into force under the Drivers Hours (Passenger Vehicles) (Modifications) Order 1970, and in anticipation of these extensive alterations to services and reduction in frequencies took place on 9 March 1970. Following the discontinuation of the Huddersfield Corporation trolleybus service from West Vale to Huddersfield, its former operation was co-ordinated with the Halifax - Huddersfield

Painted in the orange, green & cream livery of its new owner Calderdale Joint Omnibus Committee, ex.Todmorden JOC East Lancs-bodied Leyland Leopard 335 (520BWT) stands in Todmorden bus station. *T.Worsnop collection*

Taking a break in Powell Street, Halifax is NCME-bodied Daimler Fleetline 92 (MJX12J), one of seven bought new by the Corporation in 1970. *K.A.Jenkinson collection*

bus service (43) to form a new service (42) between the two towns via West Vale, giving a combined frequency of 15 minutes and a subsequent reallocation of vehicle duties between the Halifax and Huddersfield JOCs. Additionally the Sowerby Bridge - Elland OMO service was also to be operated via West Vale and Saddleworth Road. Other changes involved services 3 and 4 to Northowram with the latter being extended from the Yew Tree Inn to Northowram Hospital and both being converted to double deck operation, the transfer of the Mytholmroyd terminus of the Cragg Vale (53) service from Caldene Avenue to Bankfield operating on a circular basis and the linking of the Heptonstall (46) and Brighouse via Southowram (50) services. Later, on 2 July the availability of concessionary fares was altered to start at 9.00am instead of 9.30am.

The first new buses to enter service during 1970 did so at the start of February when the Corporation put into use NCME-bodied Daimler Fleetline double decker 94 (LJX404H) and the JOC added 2 buses of this type to its fleet (291/2 : LJX403/2H), the first of which was the replacement for the bus bearing the same number which had been sent to South Africa by Transport Vehicles (Daimler) Ltd. during the previous year.

Regretfully, on 4 August 1970 an unofficial stoppage took place following the employment of the undertaking's first female driver, Miss Sandra Holt, with buses being abandoned in the town centre during the course of the morning. Being then temporarily suspended until the Trades Union agreed to her appointment, she ultimately resumed her driving duties on 24 August. However, the first ever full day strike of traffic staff took place on 25 September over a national pay claim. Meanwhile, widespread changes in service frequencies took place on 24 August, particularly in the evenings and on Sundays with reductions and withdrawals affecting all except 13 of the undertaking's routes. Surprisingly, however, evening services on the Washer Lane and Claremount routes which had been withdrawn in March were reinstated. All journeys on the Siddal route were altered to operate via Bailey Hall, with all those running via Water Lane being cancelled, whilst the Copley service started to operate via Shaw Hill, the Railway Station and Horton Street instead of along Heath Road and Skircoat Road.

The next new buses to be received by the JOC broke new ground in being Seddon RU single deckers fitted with Plaxton dual-purpose bodywork. Numbered 315-7 (MJX15-7J), the first entered service in October with the other two following a month later. During December, the Corporation added a further 7 NCME-bodied Daimler Fleetline double deckers to its fleet (87-93 : MJX14J & MJX8-13J). Earlier in the year, in April three of the JOC's 1960 AEC Regent Vs (211/2/8) were loaned to Hebble Motor Services following the transfer of six of the Corporation's

AEC Regent Vs to the JOC a month earlier, and upon their return in September the JOC withdrew its 5 Dennis Lolines due to a reduction in private hire activities and the fact that they were not suitable for one-man-operation.

In July 1930 Hebble Bus Services, which had been bought outright by the LMS and LNE Railway Companies in May 1929, was reformed by its owners together with the British Electric Traction Company Limited as Hebble Motor Services Ltd. and two years later, on 22 February 1932, the JOCs 'C' services were transferred to it. Although its fleet, which largely comprised Albion PM-types, Leyland PLSC Lions and Leyland TD1s had by this time fallen from 72 to 60 buses but increased again when the company took over the Rochdale route from the LMS later in 1932. In August 1935 its Rochdale and Burnley routes were joined to that from Halifax to Leeds to provide a through service and after the war a series of takeovers included Brearley Tours, Ripponden & District and Walton & Helliwell (owned by O. & C. Holdsworth who were the founders of the Hebble company).

All the bus interests of the British Electric Traction Co. were sold to the state-owned Transport Holding Company from 1 March 1968 and on 1 January 1969 the newly-formed National Bus Company took over all the THC's interests. As a consequence, the three former BET companies in the area - Hebble Motor Services, West Riding Automobile Co. and Yorkshire Woollen District Transport were placed under the control of West Riding at Wakefield and as part of a rationalisation plan, Hebble took over the operation of Yorkshire Woollen's Halifax - Leeds (direct) and Halifax - Leeds via Cleckheaton services together with 7 double and 2 single deck buses. Not long afterwards, Hebble's Halifax - Bingley service

Fitted with a route board below its side windows, JOC dual-purpose seated Plaxton-bodied AEC Reliance 261 (OJX61K) leaves Crossfield bus station on its way to Leeds. As can be seen, it was painted in a cream livery with orange band and green window surrounds and roof.
K.A.Jenkinson collection

Passing through Great Horton on its way from Bradford to Halifax via Queensbury, NCME-bodied AEC Regent V 366 (RCP237) was acquired by the Corporation from Hebble Motor Services in April 1971 and passed to Calderdale JOC in June 1972. As can be seen, its illuminated side advert panel appropriately carried the message 'It's best by bus'. *J.Fozard*

was integrated into that maintained by Yorkshire Woollen from Ossett to Keighley as well as taking over Yorkshire Woollen's share of the Bradford - Halifax - Manchester express service. As a result of these changes, the Hebble fleet reached its all time high of 136 vehicles in 1970 from a mere 70 in 1968, this increase causing all kinds of problems at its Walnut Street depot at Halifax with excess vehicles requiring space in the nearby cattle market grounds. Meanwhile, Hebble's Park Lane depot at Bradford had closed on 31 October 1969 after which its allocation was temporarily housed at NBC subsidiary West Yorkshire Road Car Co's depot in the city until the latter took over its services (Bradford - Wilsden and Bradford - Huddersfield) on 2 May 1970 following the return to Yorkshire Woollen of the Halifax - Leeds and Bradford - Manchester routes.

As stated earlier, on 1 January 1969 the former responsibilities of the British Railways Board in the Halifax, Huddersfield, Sheffield and Todmorden Joint Omnibus Committees also passed to the National Bus Company who re-activated the dormant Nottinghamshire and Derbyshire Traction Co. Ltd. as the Amalgamated Passenger Transport Co. Ltd. for this purpose, its headquarters being at the Saville Town, Dewsbury offices of Yorkshire Woollen District Transport. From July 1969 all the railway owned buses of the four JOCs were licensed to A.P.T.Limited and after Huddersfield and Sheffield Corporations had purchased A.P.T's share of their undertakings, Halifax Corporation also indicated in November 1969 its intention to do likewise and also acquire certain of Hebble Motor Services' routes and vehicles following receipt of a letter from the Department of the Environment on the need to co-ordinate services in particular areas. The negotiations were not, however,

immediately opened by A.P.T. and consequently rationalisation of two services between Halifax and Bradford (via Shelf and Queensbury) by Halifax JOC, Hebble Motor Services and Bradford City Transport was seen to be the answer, with resulting savings of buses. As this would have required an amendment to the agreement of 1929, so as to enable Halifax JOC vehicles to operate on routes to Bradford, at a meeting of the JOC on 16 December 1970 the proposed merger was preferred by the parties concerned, affecting certain stage carriage interests of Hebble Motor Services and other assets, with a view to improving bus services within the Calder Valley area and reducing uneconomic operational costs of maintaining separate and often parallel services of the two undertakings. Preparations were duly made for this by the transfer of 7 surplus vehicles from the Corporation to the JOC from 1 January 1971.

The Leeds via Dudley Hill, drastically reduced Burnley via Blackshaw Head, Rochdale, and Cleckheaton services were taken over on 22 February 1971 with that to Leeds (route 8) now being terminated at Halifax with no through working and the 15 to Burnley only operating through at certain times. The latter and the Heptonstall JOC service 46, severed from the Brighouse - Southowram section at Halifax, were replaced by Blackshaw Head journeys (route 16) which on both 15 and 16 journeys operated through Heptonstall Village on the outward journey and called at the village on its return before proceeding to Slack Bottom. The Rochdale service ran over two routes, retaining no.28 for that via Ripponden while no.27 was given to the alternative route between Triangle and Gig Mill to serve Mill Bank, replacing the Mill Bank service pioneered by Ripponden & District Motors as well as the same company's infrequent Halifax to

Standing in Crossfield bus station, Halifax is 305 (5875W), a Burlingham-bodied Leyland Leopard acquired in January 1971 from Hebble Motor Services. *H.W.Peers*

Park Royal-bodled AEC Reliance 320 (BJX134C) seen here at Catherine Street, Elland, was one of a number of buses inherited by the Joint Omnibus Committee from Hebble Motor Services in March 1971. *N.Harris*

Seen at Towngate, Southowram soon after being acquired by the Corporation from Hebble Motor Services, Alexander-bodled AEC Reliance 123 (PCP803) still wore its former owner's livery and fleet number when caught by the camera in April 1971. *N.Harris*

Although still sporting the livery of their previous owner Todmorden JOC, all-Leyland PD2/1 HWY36 and MCCW-bodled Leyland Tiger Cub YAL366 had already gained Calderdale Joint Omnibus Committee fleet numbers 351 and 340 respectively when they were photographed at Portsmouth terminus in April 1971. *N.Harris*

Ordered by Halifax but delivered new to West Yorkshire PTE, Plaxton-bodled Leyland Leopard 8512 (JWU255N) stands alongside sister bus 8528 (RWT528R) in its Yorkshire Rider days. *K.A.Jenkinson*

Delivered new to Calderdale Joint Omnibus Committee in 1972, NCME-bodied Daimler Fleetline 299 (RCP279K) passes Millwood depot, Todmorden on a journey to Portsmouth when only a few days old. *J.Fozard*

Ripponden via Mill Bank and Bee Hive. The Cleckheaton service (40) and its closely linked counterpart (38) Cleckheaton - Scholes became the first example of Yorkshire Woollen District/Halifax JOC joint operation and took Halifax buses to Cleckheaton for the first time. The remaining changes took place on 1 March 1970 when the Ossett - Keighley/Bingley services of Yorkshire Woollen District were split at Halifax and the Halifax - Keighley and Halifax - Bingley portions were taken over by Halifax JOC. Hebble's two Halifax - Bradford services both disappeared on this date when they were replaced by a joint operation between Halifax JOC and Bradford City Transport, the 77 service via Shelf being extended in Halifax to the General Hospital at this same time and thus replacing Corporation service 4 from the General Hospital to Northowram Hospital while the 76 service via Queensbury allowed JOC service 40 from Halifax to Queensbury to be withdrawn. Also replaced were the Bradford City Transport services to Shelf and Queensbury and the infrequent Hebble service from Halifax to Bradford via Wibsey was withdrawn without replacement. The other Hebble services - Bradford - Hipperholme via Coley and via Lumbrook continued as services 71 and 70 with an extension from Hipperholme to Brighouse via the Stoney Lane estate, supplementing the 47 route between the estate and Brighouse which was revised to operate via Waterloo Road and Halifax Road over the last mile or so in Brighouse.

Amongst the other changes to the route network on 1 March was the commencement of a new circular service in the Illingworth area through the Abbey Park estate, linking with the existing 20, 21 and 22 routes, the conversion to OMO of route 26 (Newlands/Warley - Halifax - Bradshaw) which was extended through Queensbury to Hunger Hill estate and replaced the 27 Halifax - Bradshaw - Queensbury and 33 Halifax - Shibden - Queensbury services and the extension of certain journeys on route 59 (Elland - Ripponden) to Gig Mill to connect with the Halifax - Rochdale route (27). A number of other services were renumbered as a result of these changes and additionally the Halifax - King Cross - Norton Tower service was withdrawn except for one journey each way.

A total of 20 additional vehicles were required by the JOC to operate these services, 10 of which were to be provided by the JOC and 10 by Hebble Motor Services and to this end the Corporation transferred 5 Roe-bodied Daimler CVG6s, 2 Weymann-bodied Leyland PD2/37s and 3 Weymann-bodied Leyland Leopards to the JOC while Hebble transferred only 9 vehicles (3 Burlingham-bodied Leyland Leopards, 3 Park Royal-bodied AEC Reliances and 1 Metro Cammell and 2 Weymann-bodied AEC Regent Vs). In addition, the JOC also received 2 Burlingham-bodied Leyland Leopards from Yorkshire Woollen District Transport. As a temporary measure, an AEC Regent V

The only Alexander-bodied double decker ever to be included in the Halifax fleets was Daimler Fleetline 103 (BHD222C) which was acquired from Yorkshire Woollen District Transport in August 1971 and is seen here at the bus park close to Crossfield bus station. *T.Worsnop*

Seen at Todmorden bus station a few days before being taken over by Calderdale Joint Omnibus Committee, Todmorden JOC's 1969 Pennine-bodied Leyland Leopard 23 (BWU693H) prepares to undertake a football special to **Burnley.** *K.A.Jenkinson collection.*

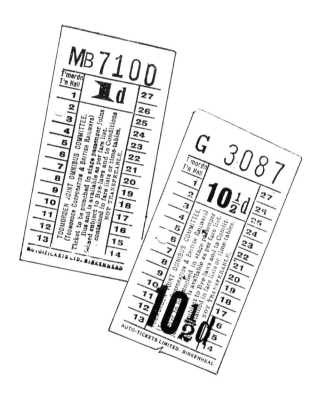

Amongst the buses taken over from Todmorden JOC by Calderdale Joint Omnibus Committee upon its formation in September 1971 was all-Leyland PD2/12 356 (KWX18) which is seen here in Orange Street, Halifax after gaining its new owner's orange, green & cream livery. *J.Fozard*

One of a trio of ECW-bodied Leyland Leopard coaches purchased by Todmorden JOC from Sheffield JOC in 1970, 1882WA is seen here at Todmorden bus station after passing to the new Calderdale JOC in September 1971. Painted in its new owner's cream, orange & green dual purpose/coach livery, it displays its new fleet number - 323 - below its windscreens. *K.A.Jenkinson collection*

double deckers was borrowed by the JOC from Hebble from February to April as were 3 AEC Reliance single deckers during March. Although a substantial number of Hebble staff were given employment by the JOC, its depot at Walnut Street was not included in the deal and was instead closed.

Prior to the above changes taking place, the first Halifax area 'buses only' lane, a contraflow along part of Waterhouse Street, came into use on 4 January 1971 and the first ever subsidy for a particular service of the undertaking commenced on 27 January when Hebden Royd Urban District Council approved a sum of money in support of the 10.10pm journey from Mytholmroyd to Cragg Vale and return. Also introduced was an increased and converted fare scale with the controversial decision not to use the new 1/2p upon the changeover to decimal currency on 21 February.

Talks had also begun in 1969 with Todmorden Corporation with a view to effecting a merger of the two Joint Committees, but the matter was deferred at the request of the Todmorden authority. However, after a period of reflection the talks were reactivated on 17 March 1971, and a month later the two Borough Councils ratified in principle the idea that the two Joint Committees should join together at an early date. This was brought a stage nearer on 12 April 1971 when, upon the retirement of Mr.W.E.Metcalfe, General Manager of the Todmorden Joint Omnibus Committee for 26 years, Geoffrey Hilditch, General Manager and Engineer of the Halifax undertaking assumed the responsibility of Acting Manager of the Todmorden JOC pending the completion of the merger agreement. Although this was not concluded until the autumn, the Todmorden fleet was almost immediately renumbered into the Halifax series, this task being completed by 6 May and thereafter

Three of the buses repainted into experimental liveries immediately prior to the formation of West Yorkshire PTE are seen here in their short-lived colour schemes, none of which were adopted by the new undertaking. Weymann-bodied Leyland PD2/37 68 (DCP68D) in George Street is followed by standard Halifax-liveried MCCW-bodied Leyland PD3/4 204 (KCP13) while Corporation MCCW-bodied Leyland PD2/37 25(MJX25) is seen in Crossley Street. Picking up its passengers at Stump Cross on its way from Brighouse to Halifax is NCME-bodied Daimler Fleetline 105 (ECP685D). *N.Harris*

Standing in King Edward Street, Halifax soon after its transfer from Metro Huddersfield to Calderdale in August 1974 Roe-bodied Leyland PD3A/2 421 (WVH421) was initially operated in Huddersfield Corporation livery. *J.Sharp*

Top left : **Plaxton Pointer-bodied Dennis Dart demonstrator N305DHE passes along Wade House Road, Shelf whilst working the 534 service on 3 August 1996.**
B.Newsome

Top right : **Leyland National 2 1322 (LUA322V) in Metrobus livery is seen here on a private hire duty.**
G.R.Littlewood

Centre : **Painted in PTE Verona green & buttermilk livery but having its Metrobus fleet name covered by a Yorkshire Rider Todmorden vinyl, ex.Calderdale JOC NCME-bodied Fleetline 3305 (RCP335K) stands outside Milwood depot.**
K.A.Jenkinson

Bottom left : **Painted all-over jonquil prior to receiving its green relief, Yorkshire Rider Roe-bodied Fleetline 7033 leaves Horton Bank Top on its way from Halifax to Bradford in September 1986.**
K.A.Jenkinson

Bottom right : **Wearing Yorkshire Rider colours and with Halifax district fleet names, Roe-bodied Leyland Olympian 5020 (UWW20X) departs from Halifax bus station on a schools service.** *K.A.Jenkinson*

Todmorden JOC added four dual-purpose Willowbrook-bodied Leyland Leopards to its fleet in 1967, one of which was NWW91E. Seen at Todmorden bus station in 1973 after its absorption into the Calderdale JOC fleet, it had received its new owner's fleet number 327 and cream, orange & green livery.
J.Fozard

the interchange of buses became commonplace whenever the necessity arose.

After the idea of building a tramway had been discarded as a result of the cost of track and overhead equipment, Todmorden Corporation took over the horse bus operations of the Todmorden and District Carriage Company and began three new services using motor omnibuses on 1 January 1907. These ran from the Town Hall to Cornholme, to Hebden Bridge and to the 'Wagon & Horses' between Walsden and Summit and a year later, a new bus depot was built on the fringe of the town at Millwood. Its original fleet comprised 2 Critchley-Norris, 1 Ryknield and 2 Leyland U-type double deckers which were painted in a livery of olive green and cream and were joined in 1909 by 2 more double deckers (a Crossley-Leyland and a Critchley-Norris), both of which were purchased secondhand. From 1913, however, apart from 2 more Critchley-Norris double deckers, a Straker Squire and a Karrier, all of which were bought secondhand in 1915/8, until its demise in 1971 Todmorden standardised on Leyland products without exception. It was not until after World War I that Todmorden Corporation added any further services to its original three, but then, during the 'twenties it gradually expanded its network in 1923 with two routes running to Burnley (one via Cornholme, the other via Bacup). In 1925 its Hebden Bridge service was extended to Oxenhope and a year later a new local route was inaugurated to Walsden and Lumbutts. 1927 saw the Oxenhope service extended onward to Keighley while finally, in 1928, a peak-hours limited stop service was introduced to Rochdale jointly with Rochdale Corporation.

Negotiations with the LMS Railway Company commenced in 1929 and resulted in the formation of the Todmorden Joint Omnibus Committee with effect from 1 January 1931, and on that date half of the fleet was sold to the Railway Company with the other half remaining under Corporation ownership. The history of the Todmorden Joint Committee is almost identical to that of Halifax JOC in that the LMS Railway Company interest passed to the British Transport Commission (later British Railways Board) on 1 January 1947 and then to the National Bus Company on its formation on 1 January 1969 who placed it under the control of the Amalgamated Passenger Transport Co. Ltd.

At a meeting of the recently formed Calderdale Joint Steering Committee held in Halifax on 29 July 1971, a new organisation was set up under the title of Calderdale Joint Omnibus Committee and included amongst its composition were two members elected by Todmorden Council, with a revised member allocation for the Amalgamated Passenger Transport Co. and Halifax Corporation according to respective fleet proportions. Vehicles and financial apportionments were also to be on the basis of 68 parts National Bus Company, 13 parts Todmorden and 55 parts Halifax Corporation out of a total of 136 parts, this being the initial authorised fleet establishment. The merger was duly completed on 6 September 1971 and from this date the Halifax and Todmorden Joint Omnibus Committees ceased to operate public service vehicles, and the first formal meeting of the new Committee took place, in Ripon, on 30 September. The offices of the Millwood depot at Todmorden were closed and its staff transferred to either Halifax at Skircoat Road or the Todmorden bus station office while the adjoining workshop at the side of the depot was not taken over but the Phoenix works across the road was rented from Todmorden Corporation as was Millwood depot. The livery of the new Joint Committee's vehicles was to be identical to that of the Halifax undertaking (i.e. orange, green and cream) but with the omission of the Halifax coat-of-arms and instead, Calderdale ownership being indicated on the legal lettering panel of the buses concerned.

The final outcome of the merger was the second major service reorganisation to occur within six months when, on 27 September 1971, the routes previously operated by Todmorden JOC were largely incorporated within those of the Halifax undertaking. Thus, the main changes in the Todmorden area affected the following services :

8   Halifax - Leeds. Extended to operate through to Burnley on an hourly frequency, stopping only at fare stages between Todmorden and Northowram together with main stops in Halifax town centre and at Stump Cross.
15 Halifax - Blackshaw Head - Burnley. Reduction in the number of through journeys.

Parked up at Skircoat Road depot are a trio of Leyland Leopards which originated from companies whose operations were taken over in 1971. Burlingham-bodied 308 (on the left) joined the Halifax JOC fleet from Yorkshire Woollen District Transport whilst sister 309 (on the right) came from Hebble Motor Services. In the centre, ECW-bodied 322 (1881WA) was one of the vehicles taken over by Calderdale JOC from Todmorden JOC and ironically all three originated with Sheffield JOC.   *H.W.Peers*

Seen in the yard of Elmwood depot after their passage to West Yorkshire PTE in April 1974 are Halifax's two AEC Matador heavy recovery vehicles and Weymann-bodied Leyland Leopard 3233 (PJX233), all of which still wear their former owner's colours. *J.Sharp*

18 Keighley - Hebden Bridge - Todmorden. Former Todmorden JOC route extended from Hebden Bridge to Todmorden and operated jointly with West Yorkshire Road Car Co. Ltd.

44 Halifax - Todmorden. Discontinued and number reused for Todmorden - Halifax Hospital service.

53 Cragg Vale (former Halifax JOC) section linked to former Todmorden JOC route between Hebden Bridge and Old Town.

90 Halifax - Todmorden - Summit.

91 Halifax - Todmorden - Cross Lee.

92 Halifax - Todmorden - Portsmouth
Three co-ordinated double deck routes with through Calder Valley fares introduced, replacing former Todmorden JOC routes and Halifax - Hebden Bridge part of the former Halifax JOC Brighouse - Hebden Bridge service.

93 Todmorden - Cloughfoot - Sharneyford. Through journeys reintroduced to Bacup.

94. Todmorden - Walsden - Mankinholes. Former Todmorden JOC route.

95 Todmorden - Rochdale. Former Todmorden JOC route, Saturdays only extended to Burnley.

97 Portsmouth - Todmorden - Walsden. Peak hour cross-Todmorden service.

Changes affecting other services in Halifax from 27 September 1971 were :

3 Halifax - Bradshaw - Hunger Hill. Converted to single deck OMO.

10 Halifax - Shibden - Northowram. Extended from Northowram Hospital to Stephens Close, allowing the virtual withdrawal of route 73.

21 Halifax - Pavement Lane. To operate via Crossley Street and Crosshills instead of via the bus station and Corporation Street.

26 Warley - Halifax - Bradshaw. Reverted to double deck operation.

27/28 Rochdale - Halifax. Extended to Leeds, stopping at fare stages between King Cross and Northowram as well as in Halifax town centre and Stump Cross. 27 service travels via Foxen Lane instead of Crabfield and Lumbridge, Soyland. An additional journey on former Mill Bank route from Sowerby Bridge, commencing at Halifax to Ripponden and extended to Dean Head, subsidised by Ripponden UDC on a 50-50 basis with Calderdale JOC, taking into account the fares received.

36 Halifax - Paddock Lane. All day joint operation with Yorkshire Woollen District Transport.

48/49 Hebden Bridge - Brighouse. Truncated to operate between Halifax and Brighouse only.

79 Whinney Hill Estate - Brighouse - Field Lane Estate. New OMO service to present terminus of service 51 at Nunnery Lane.

Route numbers shown in bold figures were new services.

Prior to the above reshuffle of services, an interesting development took place on 14 August when the Elland - Upper Edge, Rastrick Yorkshire Woollen District Transport service in the evenings was taken over by the JOC (worked now by Yorkshire Traction during the day), and thus 37 years after trying, unsuccessfully, to take over the former Elland-based Slater business and services, JOC buses actually operated on one of its former routes for the first time.

With the formation on 6 September of Calderdale JOC, all the former Todmorden and Halifax JOCs fleets were on this date transferred to the new body. Those from Todmorden JOC comprised 7 double deckers and 20 single deckers of which 4 of the Leyland PD2s and 2 Leyland Tiger Cubs were immediately withdrawn without being used by their new operator. Halifax JOC's contribution to the new Calderdale JOC was 9 coaches, 44 bus and dual-purpose seated single deckers and 61 double deckers, included amongst which were an NCME-bodied Daimler Fleetline acquired by the JOC from Yorkshire Woollen District, a Corporation NCME-bodied Daimler Fleetline and 2 Marshall-bodied Leyland Leopards from Yorkshire Traction in August 1971 and 4 Plaxton-bodied AEC Reliances which had been purchased new in June and August. The Corporation also acquired a number of secondhand buses in April 1971 in the form of 2 AEC Regent Vs and a pair of AEC Reliances from Hebble Motor Services from whom they had been on loan since 1 March, and an Alexander-

Acquired by Calderdale JOC from Maidstone & District in January 1972, lowbridge Park Royal-bodied AEC Regent V 364 (VKR37) was allocated to Todmorden depot where it is seen still wearing the dark green & cream colours of its former owner in May 1972, a couple of weeks prior to its withdrawal from service. *R.F.Mack*

bodied Daimler Fleetline double decker from Yorkshire Woollen District Transport in August. Finally, in December, a further Marshall-bodied Leyland Leopard was purchased by Calderdale JOC from Yorkshire Traction whilst an order placed by Halifax for 10 more Seddon RUs was cancelled on grounds that they would not qualify for the Government's bus grant.

Before the year ended, Hepton Rural District Council decided on 9 December to subsidise a shopping service between Hardcastle Crags and Hebden Bridge on Thursday afternoons while back in Halifax, work was now proceeding on an extension to the undertaking's Elmwood depot to accommodate a new tyre store and repair shop. 1971 had been, without doubt, the most dramatic year in Halifax's transport history since the war, and indeed since 1929, and there was more to follow.

On the first day of 1972, as a result of the late delivery of new vehicles, Calderdale JOC placed in service 4 AEC Regent V double deckers purchased from Maidstone & District Motor Services. Fitted with rear entrance Park Royal bodies which incorporated platform doors, two of these buses were of lowbridge configuration whilst the other two were of the normal highbridge type and all retained their former operator's livery of dark green and cream. The two lowbridge examples were allocated to Todmorden depot (which could not accommodate normal height double deckers), but due to being equipped with small AEC 7.7 litre engines, all four buses were confined mainly to peak-hours rather than all-day duties. Being acquired only as a stop-gap measure, all four were withdrawn at the end of May upon the arrival of 17 new NCME-bodied Daimler Fleetlines of which 12 (295-306 : RCP282/3/77-81/332-6K) were allocated to the JOC fleet and the remaining 5 (82-6 : RCP272-6K) to the Corporation. Later in the year, in October, the Corporation also benefited from the arrival of 5 new Plaxton-bodied Leyland Leopards (1-5 : SCP341-5L), these replacing 4 Leyland Royal Tiger Worldmasters and 2 AEC Regent Vs which had been transferred to the JOC in June..

With effect from 3 January 1972, an increased service subsidised by Sowerby Bridge and Ripponden UDCs was introduced on the Mill Bank (24) service with the shopping bus to Ripponden also restored while route 27 (Halifax - Rochdale) reverted to operating via Lighthazels instead of Foxen Lane, and on the same day the 79 service from Brighouse to Nunnery Lane was altered to operate via Oaklands, replacing the 52 Brighouse -

Oaklands route. Later, on 31 January, as a result of a co-ordination agreement with West Yorkshire Road Car Co. the two-hourly service between Halifax and Bingley (route 1) was withdrawn and on the following day a two-hourly service from Halifax to Keighley (route 2) was started in its place. Also on this same day West Yorkshire Road Car Co. was given a one bus allocation on the 70/1 Bradford - Hipperholme - Brighouse routes.

After much discussion with the Trades Unions, double deck one-man-operation began on 9 October 1972 on the Corporation Pellon, Savile Park circular routes and the JOC services from Halifax to Brighouse via Slead Syke and Bonegate, Brighouse to Field Lane and Brighouse to Stoney Lane, thus paving the way for future developments. A month afterwards, reductions, particularly at weekends and evenings, took place on the Blackley, Dean Head and Blackshaw Head routes from 20 November whilst a new Wednesdays and Fridays only service (numbered 98) was started between the Carr House estate and Todmorden. In addition, the Halifax to Midgley and Booth services were both diverted to operate through the Kershaw Estate at Luddendenfoot to compensate for the withdrawal of the service from the Estate to Sowerby Bridge and the Beechwood Road service was replaced by the Hunger Hill via Bradshaw route which was changed to run through the estate instead of directly along Shay Lane from Ovenden.

After starting quietly, 1973 got underway on 31 March when the representatives of the Amalgamated Passenger Transport Co. on Calderdale Joint Omnibus Committee indicated their intention of terminating the previous JOC agreements (May 1929 and September 1971) on 31 March 1974 in view of the anticipated merger of municipal undertakings on 1 April 1974 to form the West Yorkshire Passenger Transport Executive. This was not unexpected in view of the possibility of the need to meet a serious financial deficit at the end of the current financial year and prompted the Corporation to agree at the appropriate time to make an application for certain licences held by the JOC.

Cutbacks in services, particularly in the Elland/Greetland areas, finally came on 2 April 1973 when the Elland - Ripponden service was withdrawn and replaced by two new circular routes (58/9) from Elland (Catherine Street) via West Vale, Saddleworth Road, Brian Royd Lane, Greetland and Rochdale Road back to Elland in both directions. Certain journeys on the Halifax - Barkisland service were extended to Ripponden and all Norland journeys continued to Barkisland with some proceeding onward to Krumlin and Ringstone in order to replace the old 59 service. The Elland - Sowerby Bridge service was withdrawn at off-peak times but Exley Lane had its service restored with two workings while a new service, numbered 69, was introduced between Elland and Blackley. The Halifax - Outlane (direct) service 38 was withdrawn completely and the 43 service between Halifax and Huddersfield via Elland Wood Bottom was also withdrawn (after almost fifty years of operation) with all buses now following the 42 service to West Vale then the 42 to Elland via Long Wall or 43 to Elland via Bank Bottom. Other changes included a reduction in the subsidised service 24 (Halifax - Mill Bank), the withdrawal of limited stop facilities from the Burnley - Leeds service (8) in the evenings, and a reduction in the Cragg Vale - Old Town service, although this was not as drastic as had been expected due to the continued support from Hebden Royd UDC, West Riding County Council and the Department of the Environment.

The Elland - Sowerby Bridge route frequency was, however, improved following a bid by Travelways of Halifax, a private coach operator, to operate the route in June 1973 but the Elland - Exley service was not so fortunate and was withdrawn on 13 August when the Elland - Blackley service was proportionately increased to compensate. Later in the year, on 1 October revisions were made to the Calder Valley services with the discontinuation of the through running of the Leeds - Burnley route (8) and the extension of the Halifax - Portsmouth service (92) through to Burnley. At this same time the Burnley - Portsmouth - Littleborough service (95) was amended to run on an hourly frequency and the Halifax - Summit route (90) was extended to Littleborough while at the end of the year a new service was commenced between Todmorden and the Longfield estate.

By now, preparations were well in hand for the formation of the West Yorkshire Passenger Transport Executive from the Halifax, Huddersfield, Bradford and Leeds undertakings and on 30 November Corporation Weymann-bodied Leyland PD2/37 68 (DCP68D) was repainted into an experimental scheme of

Shortly before the West Yorkshire PTE took over the operations and vehicles of the various municipal and JOC undertakings in the county, a number of experimental new liveries were applied to Halifax buses before the decision was taken to standardise on the Verona green & buttermilk scheme. Amongst these were various applications of green & cream, two of which are illustrated on Corporation NCME-bodied Daimler Fleetlines 99 (ECP679D) in Waterhouse Street, Halifax and 100 (ECP680D) at Crossfield bus station. As can be seen, both buses sport experimental Metro Calderdale fleet names.
K.A.Jenkinson collection

buttermilk with orange relief, yellow door, red wheels and black mudguards and was fitted with 'Metro Calderdale' fleet names and PTE logos. It was initially suggested that buses in each of the PTE's districts should have some of their municipalities original colours incorporated into the unifying buttermilk scheme adopted by the PTE, but in the event 68's livery proved unsuccessful and was consequently not adopted. In February 1974, however, further livery experiments were undertaken when Corporation

The last new buses to be delivered to the Corporation before the West Yorkshire PTE took over its operations were five Plaxton-bodied Leyland Leopards. One of these, 9 (UJX919M) is seen at Crossfield bus station prior to its departure on the cross-Pennines service to Rochdale via Mill Bank and Littleborough.
K.A.Jenkinson collection

Daimler Fleetlines 99/100/5 (ECP679/80/5D), Calderdale JOC Leyland Leopard 326 (NNW90E) and Leyland PD2/37 25 (MJX25) were all repainted into dark green and buttermilk schemes, but these too were rejected and as will be seen later, when the PTE came into being, it adopted a corporate livery which was applied to all its buses, irrespective of the areas in which they operated.

The last new buses to be delivered to Halifax Corporation made their debut in November and December 1973 in the form of 5 more Plaxton-bodied Leyland Leopards (6-10 : UJX916-20M) while in December Calderdale JOC received 3 more low-height NCME-bodied Daimler Fleetlines (309-11 : VCP839-41M), these being joined by a further pair (307/8 : VCP837/8M) early in 1974 with 308 having the honour of being the last bus to enter service with the JOC when it took up its duties in February. The final inter-fleet transfers took also took place at this time when 5 Leyland Royal Tiger Worldmasters moved from the Corporation to the JOC in January 1974 and a Leyland Leopard went in the opposite direction in February.

As the end of the Halifax undertaking now rapidly approached, the final major event in its history took place on 1 March 1973 when a new bus station was opened in Brighouse, replacing the previous terminal, the land upon which it stood being required for redevelopment. With the service network and Corporation and JOCs fleets experiencing no further changes, March 31 was eventually reached, and after a period of almost 76 years of municipal transport operation and exactly 45 years of joint bus operation, the Halifax undertaking passed into the annals of history. In its final twelve months of operation, approximately 53 million tickets were issued and its 200 buses, both Corporation and JOC, ran approximately 8 million miles, the equivalent to each bus travelling two and a half times round the earth, using 900,000 gallons of diesel fuel, with a total staff of 800. Although Halifax's transport undertaking now no longer existed, its attractive orange, green and cream livery was to soldier on for a few years longer, however, and did not disappear completely until all the buses wearing it were either withdrawn from service or gained their new owner's colours in their normal repainting cycle.

THE NEW PTE TAKES CONTROL

On 1 April 1974 the West Yorkshire Passenger Transport Executive came into being as part of the changes in local government and the creation of the West Yorkshire Metropolitan County Council whose powers included the planning and provision of passenger transport throughout its area. The new Passenger Transport Executive was set up as a means of fulfilling these new responsibilities in accordance with the policies laid down by the Public Transport Committee of the Metropolitan County Council, and although these encompassed all the bus operators in West Yorkshire including the former Halifax, Huddersfield, Bradford and Leeds municipal undertakings and Calderdale Joint Omnibus Committee, only those which affected Halifax are briefly chronicled in the following paragraphs, as to include them all would require a separate volume.

With effect from 1 April 1974, the 223 vehicles previously operated by Halifax Corporation and Calderdale Joint Omnibus Committee passed to the PTE and were renumbered into its new scheme by having 3000 added to their existing fleet numbers. Repainting into the PTE's corporate Verona green and buttermilk livery began immediately as did the fitting of new Metro Calderdale fleet names to all the Halifax-based vehicles and several inter-fleet transfers began to be made. Amongst the first of these was a former Bradford City Transport Daimler Fleetline whose body had been destroyed by fire soon after it had passed to the PTE. After being fitted with a new NCME body, instead of re-entering service in Bradford it was transferred to Metro

Calderdale in December 1974 despite retaining its Bradford area fleet number 2352. In the meantime, in order to concentrate all the PTE's Seddon vehicles in its Kirklees district, Halifax's 3 buses of this type (3315-7) were transferred to Huddersfield in June 1974 while Kirklees Leyland PD3A/2s 4409/10/2/3/5/7-9/21/4 moved to Halifax where they initially retained their former owner's red and cream livery. Additionally, the PTE's solitary Leyland National (1301) was transferred from Leeds to Halifax in November while former Bradford City Transport Marshall-bodied Leyland Panthers 2508-12 also moved to Halifax where they entered service in their original blue and cream colours.

Early in 1975, one of Metro Calderdale's recently-delivered Roe-bodied Leyland Atlanteans (6003) was fitted with a new Leyland G-2 automatic gearbox and was almost immediately loaned to South Yorkshire PTE for evaluation. In exchange, one of the latter's East Lancs-bodied Bristol VRTs was despatched to Halifax where it operated for two weeks commencing 3 February, mainly on the 76 and 77 services to Bradford. Later, in May the ex.Bradford Leyland Panthers were taken out of service and sold to Chesterfield Corporation while in May Calderdale received 3 of the ex.Leeds forward entrance Roe-bodied Daimler CVG6s from Kirklees. Another stranger joining the Halifax fleet was an Alexander-bodied Volvo-Ailsa double decker (3480) which was purchased by the PTE for evaluation. Although this quickly settling down on the Huddersfield service, it did not generate orders for any further buses of this type and thus remained

Seen in Carrier Street, Halifax in 1974, despite Marshall-bodied Leyland Leopard 358 (NHE8F) still wearing its orange, green & cream colours, it had already passed to West Yorkshire PTE as can be seen from its fleet number which had been prefixed with a '3'. New in 1968 to Yorkshire Traction, it had been purchased by Calderdale JOC in December 1971. *T.Worsnop*

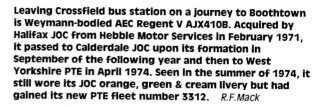

Leaving Crossfield bus station on a journey to Boothtown is Weymann-bodied AEC Regent V AJX410B. Acquired by Halifax JOC from Hebble Motor Services in February 1971, it passed to Calderdale JOC upon its formation in September of the following year and then to West Yorkshire PTE in April 1974. Seen in the summer of 1974, it still wore its JOC orange, green & cream livery but had gained its new PTE fleet number 3312.   *R.F.Mack*

Former Halifax Corporation/ Calderdale JOC Weymann-bodied Leyland Worldmaster 3372 (KCP2) painted in its new PTE Verona green & buttermilk livery makes its was over the cobbles to Crossfield bus station in October 1978 whilst working on the Siddal route.   *K.A.Jenkinson*

unique until its withdrawal and sale to Derby City Transport in April 1981.

Looking towards the future, the PTE began to examine various new type of fare collection systems in December 1975 and to this end fitted a number of its Bradford-based Leyland Atlanteans with Setright Keyspeed ticket machines and fareboxes, loaning them to Kirklees and Calderdale districts for in-service trials until the end of January 1976 when the equipment was removed and the buses concerned returned from whence they came.

In February 1976 the previous limited stop service to Leeds (8) was extended in the latter city from St.Pauls Street to the Central Bus Station and was operated jointly by Leeds and Calderdale districts using OMO double deckers and at the same time all the bus services in West Yorkshire were given individual numbers with those in Calderdale being prefixed with a figure '5'. The arrival in Halifax of a number of new low-height NCME-bodied Fleetlines enabled the conversion to one-person-operation of the Mixenden - Highroad Well and Rye Lane services with the former being extended to Norton Tower via either Court Lane or Roils Head Road. A month later, the opening of Bradford's new

The only pre-PTE buses to operate in all four of the new undertaking's districts were the forward entrance Roe-bodied Daimler CVG6s which began life with Leeds City Transport. Painted in the PTE's 'roads and pavements' style of Verona green & buttermilk livery, 872 (572CNW) stands on the bus park at Crossfield bus station during its spell with Metro Calderdale.   *T.W.W.Knowles*

Despite still wearing its orange, green & cream livery, Alexander-bodied AEC Reliance 23 (PCP803) which was acquired from Hebble Motor Services in April 1971 had already gained a Metro fleet name in May 1971 following its passage to West Yorkshire PTE a month earlier. Seen in the yard of Elmwood depot, it was being used on driver tuition duties.   *T.Worsnop*

Two former Halifax Joint Omnibus Committee Plaxton-bodied AEC Reliance coaches which passed to West Yorkshire PTE in April 1974 are seen here resting in the yard of Elmwood depot. 272 (NJX855J) still wore its original owner's orange, green & cream livery whilst 274 (KCP874G) had gained Metro's Verona green & buttermilk colours.
J.Sharp

Transport Interchange in March resulted in transfer of the two Halifax - Bradford services to this new site together with the Brighouse - Bradford services which had previously terminated at the now closed Chester Street bus station. Soon afterwards, a series of local tours similar to the previous Countryside Tours was launched by Metro Calderdale, running at Easter, Spring Bank Holiday, the Halifax holiday fortnight and Halifax Autumn Break while from 18 April an experimental Sunday park & ride service (500) was inaugurated from Hebden Bridge to Hardcastle Crags, this being supported by West Yorkshire Metropolitan County Council and Calderdale Council and using Plaxton-bodied Leyland Leopards.

As 1976 drew to a close, the district part of the fleetname began to be omitted as buses underwent repainting in order to allow the easier transfer and temporary loan of vehicles between its various operating areas and in February 1977, following the introduction of a new style of Metrobus fleet name, it was decided to simplify the corporate Verona green and buttermilk livery by extending the area of green to the whole of the lower side panels and omitting the 'roads and pavements' band above the windscreen of double deckers.

To commemorate the Silver Jubilee of H.M.Queen Elizabeth II, the PTE repainted a double decker in each of its operating districts into a special silver livery which incorporated a purple band at upper deck floor level. The Calderdale vehicle selected for this treatment was NCME-bodied Fleetline 7009, a low-height example to enable it to operate for a period from Todmorden depot, and in addition to becoming a familiar sight around Halifax for almost a year, this bus also visited Lille, Belgium from 13 to 21 April in connection with the presentation of a former Leeds City Transport Daimler CVG6 to the Lille Transport Museum (Lille being twinned with Leeds). Although Calderdale was still awaiting its new radio installation, a start was made in October on the fitting of its vehicles with two-way short wave radio equipment. This was part of the PTE's initiative to improve 'on the road' communications for drivers as well as combating the growing problem of on-bus vandalism. Prior to this, as a consequence of a two week strike by Bradford district crews which started on 2 October, although Calderdale staff voted not to join them, they agreed to terminate all their services to Bradford at the city boundary until the dispute was resolved.

With the progressive repainting of buses into the new corporate PTE livery, the old Halifax colours of orange, green and cream had been gradually phased out and on 19 March 1978 passed into the annals of history following the withdrawal on that day of Leyland PD2/37 3282, the last bus in the fleet so adorned.

Its original body being destroyed by fire in 1974, former Bradford City Transport Daimler Fleetline 2352 (XAK352L) was given a new body by NCME and in its new form was immediately transferred to Calderdale district. It is seen here in 1979 standing at the side of Elmwood depot, freshly repainted into the PTE's revised Verona green & buttermilk livery and yet to receive its Metrobus fleet name transfers. *K.A.Jenkinson*

A unique vehicle in the West Yorkshire PTE fleet was Alexander-bodied Volvo-Ailsa 3480 (LUG480P) which was purchased for evaluation and allocated to Calderdale district. Wearing its owner's revised livery which omitted the 'roads & pavements' band above its windscreen, it is seen here in 1979 descending New North Road, Huddersfield on a journey from Halifax. *K.A.Jenkinson*

Huddersfield to enable the conversion from single to double deck of a service which passed under a low railway bridge at Penistone. A few weeks later, an articulated Volvo single decker was borrowed by the PTE from Stockholm for trials on a number of services including some in Halifax, although due to its left hand drive configuration it was unable to be used in a passenger carrying capacity. Meanwhile, on 14 May Calderdale district had replaced all its remaining Ultimate ticket machines with new Almex equipment and upon the opening of the new Elland by-pass on 13 December, a number of routes in that area were diverted to make use of this new facility.

Yet another era had ended, much to the regret of many of the residents of Halifax, and the Corporation and JOC was now effectively dead. To allow the withdrawal of further Leyland PD2/37s from service in Calderdale and enable the extension of one-person-operation, 5 Daimler Fleetlines were transferred from Leeds to Halifax in June while in August 3 of Calderdale's low-height Fleetlines were transferred to Kirklees district at

1979 proved to be a somewhat uneventful year as far as Calderdale was concerned, with the only points of note being the arrival of more new NCME-bodied Fleetlines during the early part of the year and the conversion in September of the Illingworth services to one-person-operation. Similarly, 1980 was comparatively quiet, although during the spring Calderdale received 15 of the 20 new Leyland National 2s purchased by the PTE, the remaining 5 going to Kirklees. These replaced a number of the older single deckers inherited from the Corporation and JOC while at the end of July the last of the undertakings Leyland PD2/37s were withdrawn from service.

In an attempt to increase the PTE's revenue, a total of 100 double deckers were equipped with 'Sounds in Motion' equipment in their upper saloons, this involving the fitting of eight speakers through which music was played together with local advertising material. First introduced to Leeds district buses in June, the system was extended to Calderdale a few weeks later, although due to the fact that it was automatically switched on when the engine was started and that there was no choice of on or off and no volume control, this new innovation met with a mixed reception from passengers and drivers alike and was discontinued later in

The second of the Fishwick of Leyland buses borrowed by West Yorkshire PTE's Calderdale district in the autumn of 1982, Leyland National 2 OFV621X enters Northgate, Halifax enroute to Wainstalls on the 525 service. *K.A.Jenkinson*

Seen at Dean Clough, Halifax on its way to Illingworth on the 520 service in January 1982, Calderdale district Roe-bodied Fleetline 7156 (CWU156T) was adorned with posters to promote the PTE's new 30p (adult) and 15p (child) off-peak fares. *K.A.Jenkinson*

To promote the PTE's new SaverStrip tickets, several buses were repainted into a predominantly cream all-over advertising livery for this purpose. Amongst these was Calderdale district Roe-bodied Fleetline 7155 which, like all the other buses in the fleet at that time, additionally had 'Here today, gone tomorrow' vinyls applied at each side of its front destination aperture. *K.A.Jenkinson*

the year. Earlier, in March 1980 the Halifax - Bradford services which had previously been operated jointly by Bradford and Calderdale districts were reorganised so that the 681 via Shelf was worked solely by Bradford and the 576 via Queensbury only by Calderdale while in September a second 'buses only' street was opened in Halifax on the other side of Waterhouse Street from its junction with Crossley Street, northbound to Broad Street.

A number of service changes were implemented in March 1981 amongst which the 532 to Norton Tower via Warley Road and 545 Elland - Rosemount Estate routes were withdrawn along with the 558/559 Greetland - Elland and 574 Halifax -Boothtown services. In addition, the 557 and part of the 554 were replaced by a new service (540) from Halifax - Boulderclough via Tuel Lane and Sowerby Bridge while the 541 (Boulderclough - Brighouse) replaced the 541, 542 and part of the 554. At this same time the 552 became a through service between Halifax and Old Town via Hebden Bridge and the 553 (Hebden Bridge - Banksfield) was renumbered 554. Additionally, two new seasonal tourist services were inaugurated, the 500 running on Sundays and Bank Holidays between May and September from Hebden Bridge to Keighley via Oxenhope and Haworth, the 501 on Saturdays throughout the year from Todmorden to Keighley replacing the existing 589 with both being extended to Monday to Friday operation during the July and August holiday period.

On 1 January 1982 the PTE, which since its inception had been organised in five separate districts, restructured its

operations into two new divisions as part of a rationalisation plan designed to decentralise functions from Wakefield and under this reorganisation Calderdale was placed, together with Kirklees and Bradford, under the control of the new Western Division whose headquarters were established at Bradford. Soon after this change took place, Calderdale received 5 of the PTE's new type

Resting on the forecourt of Skircoat Road depot are examples of Halifax Corporation/JOC's and West Yorkshire PTE's 'standard' double deckers. On the left, former Corporation NCME-bodied Daimler Fleetline 3092 (MJX12J) was one of several buses of this type to have its three-aperture destination screen replaced by a single screen during its PTE days while Roe-bodied Leyland Fleetline 7116 (WUM116S) represents the standard body styling adopted by the PTE for its double deck fleet. *K.A.Jenkinson*

of double decker, Leyland Olympians with Roe bodywork, all of which had entered service by the early part of April, while June witnessed the arrival of a pair of new Duple Dominant IV-bodied Leyland Leopards painted in a cream, red and brown livery and sporting 'Executive' fleet names for use on private hire duties and extended tours. More unusual, however, was the appearance on 11 September of a Leyland National 2 in the livery of Fishwicks of Leyland. This was loaned to Calderdale by Leyland as a replacement for one of the PTE's own National 2s (1328) which had been returned to its manufacturer for experimental work relating to its transmission. Used mainly on the 525 (Wainstalls) route, the Fishwick vehicle was replaced by another National 2 from that same fleet early in November, and this too spent much of its time on the 525 service until its departure during late January 1983 upon the return of 1328. During the spring of 1983 a further 2 new coaches were allocated to Halifax, on this occasion Plaxton Paramount-bodied Leyland Tigers while one of Calderdale's Roe-bodied Daimler Fleetlines (7119) was painted into an all-cream livery to publicise the Bus & Coach Council campaign aimed at encouraging more people to use public transport. To further promote bus and local rail travel, on 31 July the PTE introduced a discounted ticket branded the SaverStrip, this allowing 12 journeys for the price of ten. Available from all post offices and most newsagents throughout West Yorkshire in various denominations relating to 10p, 15p, 20p, 30p, 40p, 50p and 60p single fares, these tickets were self cancelled by passengers upon boarding the bus and to this end all the PTE's vehicles had Almex SaverStrip cancelling machines fitted immediately inside their passenger entrance. Before the year ended, a further 5 new Roe-bodied Leyland Olympians were allocated to Calderdale as were 2 secondhand Duple Dominant-

bodied Leyland Leopard coaches acquired from Fox of Hayes to enhance the private hire fleet.

After extending the 503 service from Hunger Hill, Queensbury to Shelf early in 1984 to replace part of the withdrawn Yorkshire Traction service from Queensbury (Raggalds Inn) to Brighouse, the double deck operated 576 Halifax to Bradford via Queensbury service was converted to one-person-operation on 30 April. During the previous month a former London Transport DMS-type Daimler Fleetline owned by Brockhouse-Maxwell Transmissions of West Bromwich and fitted with a fully-automatic gearbox with built-in retarder was borrowed by the PTE for evaluation and although it was only used in a revenue earning capacity in Leeds, it was tested for a couple of days by Calderdale over the 576 service in a non-passenger carrying role.

Halifax, and as part of this change Greater Manchester PTE gained a working through to Halifax, bringing its buses into the town for the first time.

By now, details of the Government's new Transport Bill had been published which, if passed, would change the whole concept of bus operation throughout the country. Under the new Act, road service licensing in its present form was to be completely abolished and all subsidised services would have to be put out to competitive tender. There would be no protection from new predatory operators and thus a 'free-for-all' situation would exist where anyone could operate commercial services anywhere, provided that they were registered with the Traffic Commissioner. As a result, the PTE would lose its powers to operate bus services because of its new role managing the tendering system

Due to a temporary shortage of buses, Calderdale district borrowed a number of dual-door Roe-bodied Daimler Fleetlines from Metrobus's Leeds district for a few weeks in September 1986. One of these, 505 (JUG505L), is seen resting at the side of Elmwood depot after having worked a duty on the 547 service. *K.A.Jenkinson*

Of greater importance however, in July 1984 plans were unveiled for a new bus station in Halifax at the junction of Winding Road and Northgate, alterations to Skircoat Road depot, and the construction of a new garage at Todmorden at a total cost of almost £5 million. The Sion Chapel and Sunday School, listed building on the site, were to be incorporated in the new bus station which was to be built to a saw-tooth design with 5 platforms, 24 bus bays and lay-over parking for 17 buses. This was to replace the existing Crossfield bus station, control room, and staff canteen at Powell Street and was additionally to incorporate a travel office, shop and cafe. Although work began on the alterations to Skircoat Road depot in November, it was some time later before construction of the bus station commenced while the planned new depot at Todmorden was put on hold.

Shortly before 1984 ended, a disastrous fire in the Summit railway tunnel on 20 December led to a complete closure of the railway line between Todmorden and Rochdale and the necessity to provide a replacement bus service between these stations. For this purpose, 5 of the PTE's new coach-seated Roe-bodied Leyland Olympian double deckers (5501-5) painted in cream and brown Metrocoach livery were allocated to Calderdale and maintained this operation until 21 January 1985 when the service was truncated to operate only between Todmorden and Littleborough following the reopening of the railway line from Rochdale to Littleborough. It was not until 18 August that the tunnel at Summit was reopened, however, and the replacement bus service was able to cease. During this time, one-person-operation was further expanded with the conversion of the Huddersfield (342, 343 & 344) and Newlands - Shelf (503 & 526) services on 3 June while on 12 August the vehicle allocation of the two Halifax depots at Skircoat Road and Elmwood were combined as part of the PTE's rationalisation plans. Finally, in November the 587 service was renumbered 589 and extended from Littleborough to Rochdale as was the 590 service from

and thus the present operations would have to be formed into a single company, the ownership of which would be transferred to the PTA. In short, the prospects were daunting to say the least ....

As plans were drawn up in preparation for the implementation of the new Transport Act, the end of yet another era was marked on 19 January 1986 when conductors finally disappeared from regular services in Calderdale upon the conversion of the last remaining crew operated routes (Causeway Foot, Wainstalls, Rishworth/ Sowerby) to one-person-operation. Further changes included the introduction of 'Nightrider' services from the end of March, these running between 11.00pm and 2.30am on Fridays and Saturdays on three routes which between them served Mixenden, Ovenden, Illingworth, Elland, Brighouse, Hipperholme, Sowerby Bridge and Hebden Bridge with a flat 50p fare being charged. More important, however, was the abolition on 31 March of the West Yorkshire Metropolitan County Council as the

The PTE's coach-seated Optare-bodied Leyland Olympians were painted in an oatmeal, brown & red livery and given Metrocoach fleet names as illustrated by 5510 (C510KBT) at Elmwood depot in 1986. *K.A.Jenkinson*

Prior to gaining their new Yorkshire Rider livery, several buses were repainted overall jonquil, the bright green being added after a few weeks. Seen in this form in the yard of Elmwood depot in October 1986 soon after receiving Yorkshire Rider Halifax fleet name vinyls and legal lettering is Plaxton-bodied Leyland Leopard 8532 (RWT532R). *D.Bentley*

Passenger Transport Authority, its role being assumed from the following day by the Joint Board of District Councillors whose meetings were to be held in rotation in the five districts concerned. Meanwhile, in preparation for the implementation of the new Transport Act, a vast amount of work was being undertaken on the registration of a new commercial network of services and the calculation of tenders for those routes for which financial support was needed and in order to separate Metro's operations from the PTE two new companies were registered on 15 November under the titles West Yorkshire Metrobus Ltd. and Kirklees Buses Ltd. These were followed by the registration on 15 February 1986 by a further company, West Yorkshire Transport Company Ltd. which was renamed Yorkshire Rider Ltd. on 4 August 1986. In the meantime, to further protect its interests, several more new companies were incorporated in mid-January, these being Bradford Transport Ltd., Huddersfield Transport Ltd., Halifax Transport Ltd., Wakefield Transport Ltd. and Calderdale Transport Ltd. while added to these on 15 April was Leeds Transport Ltd. and on 1 Mat, Dartstep Ltd., the latter being renamed West Yorkshire Minibuses Ltd. on 16 July.

The only new buses to be received during the early part of 1986 were 2 of the PTE's new Optare-bodied Leyland Cub midibuses which had remained in store since their delivery in December 1985. These were used on a variety of routes but never proved popular with drivers and tended to spend much of their time in the yard of Elmwood depot rather than in revenue earning service. As a foretaste of what was to come, however, six PTE vehicles were repainted during July and August into new experimental liveries which were later adopted as standard by the newly-created Yorkshire Rider, the buses being jonquil and bright green and the coaches cream, red and gold and sporting Gold Rider fleet names. Despite approval being given to these new colours, most of the normal repaints undertaken during August and early September were in unrelieved jonquil, the bright green colour and new fleet name not being added until the final week of September. Appended to the Yorkshire Rider fleet name on all its buses was the name of the operating district, with those in Calderdale carrying either Halifax or Todmorden suffixes.

After two abortive attempts by the former Passenger Transport Authority to obtain a Section 56 grant from the Government for the construction of the new bus station, it was announced in June that the plans had now been pared down so that the cost of the project was now £1.6 million instead of the original £3 million. Although the plan still included the restoration of part of the Sion Church and the moving and resiting of the Sunday School, it no longer featured a new office block and the number of stands had been reduced from 24 to 23.

With deregulation now rapidly approaching, Yorkshire Rider placed its first minibuses in service during September, these being Optare-converted Freight Rover Sherpas. Those allocated to Halifax were initially used only on a schools contract service, although on 6 and 7 September when services 527 and 528 to Rochdale were curtailed to terminate at the Rake Inn owing to a temporary weight limit of 3.5 tons on a canal bridge at Littleborough, two were used to connect with the conventional single deckers in order to maintain the through service to Rochdale. A similar, but longer term, weight limit was applied to North Bridge, Halifax from 26 August, this causing the services normally passing over it to be diverted via Burdock Way for a number of years until the bridge was ultimately refurbished and strengthened.

D-day, 26 October 1986 finally arrived, and in addition to a large number of service changes being implemented, competition was witnessed in Halifax for the first time since 1930. Under the tendering process, Rochdale-based Yelloways Motor Services won the 556 Halifax - Oldham and 567/568 Halifax - Rochdale services while Ivy Coaches of Huddersfield won the X37 Halifax - Huddersfield limited stop route. Despite various rumours having circulated during the summer, the only competitive commercially registered services in Halifax turned out to be those registered by local independent Abbeyways between Market Street and Illingworth and Market Street and Claremount at off-peak times.

Former Halifax Corporation NCME-bodied Daimler Fleetline 3084 (RCP274K) climbs out of Great Horton on a grey February day in 1987 whilst working a 576 duty from Bradford to Halifax. Although still painted in the PTE's Verona green & buttermilk livery, its Metrobus fleet name has been covered with a Yorkshire Rider Halifax vinyl and a Welcome Aboard sticker has been added above its door. *K.A.Jenkinson*

In 1987 West Yorkshire PTE purchased 25 Carlyle-bodied Freight Rover Sherpa minibuses from West Midlands PTE, initially using them on driver training duties. Still wearing their former owner's colours, D505NDA and D502NDA are seen here resting on the bus park adjacent to Crossfield bus station, Halifax in March 1987 whilst undertaking this role. *K.A.Jenkinson*

Painted in the old Halifax orange, green & cream livery to commemorate 75 years of municipal bus operation in the town, Yorkshire Rider Roe-bodied Leyland Olympian 5096 (A98KUM) seen here at Rye Lane terminus retained these colours for ten years after becoming part of its owner's 'Building on a Great Tradition' fleet. *D.Bentley*

As a consequence of Yorkshire Rider's service alterations, its Halifax-based fleet was able to be reduced by 12 vehicles and in addition all its remaining single deckers were removed from normal service duties and confined to schools and works contracts. To replace them, 25 Roe-bodied Leyland Atlanteans were transferred from Leeds district while some low-height NCME-bodied Fleetlines returned from Kirklees and allocated to Todmorden who also received a number of Freight Rover Sherpa minibuses for operation on services in the Todmorden and Hebden Bridge areas. Meanwhile, the last remaining ex.Halifax Corporation single deckers were withdrawn for disposal while minibuses were also introduced to a new local circular service in Elland.

To commemorate the 75th anniversary of bus services in Halifax and the 80th anniversary of services in Todmorden, two Leyland Olympians were repainted into the colours of the former undertakings during the summer of 1987 with 5096 receiving the former Halifax livery of orange, green and cream and 7006 gaining Todmorden's dark green and cream. Soon after its appearance in its new colours, 5096 was loaned for eleven days to Cynon Valley Transport in South Wales (where Halifax's former General Manager Geoffrey Hilditch held a similar position) from which undertaking a Duple-bodied Leyland Tiger coach was received in exchange.

Following the disposal by the PTE of all its leased buses, Yorkshire Rider now found itself short of double deckers and in order to rectify this situation, early in September it purchased 3 NCME-bodied Fleetlines from GM Buses at Manchester, placing these in service at Halifax. Finding them suitable on the hilly services around the town, a further 50 of these were acquired between November 1987 and August 1988, all of which were allocated to Halifax where they were used to replace all the depot's Atlanteans and several of the Roe-bodied Fleetlines. Also in August 1988, Todmorden depot received 10 new low-height Northern Counties-bodied Leyland Olympians which unusually were fitted with the town's crest on their front grille despite wearing standard Yorkshire Rider livery. These replaced most of the low-height Fleetlines at the Todmorden outpost.

Freshly repainted in a jonquil livery with black skirt rather than the customary Micro Rider jonquil, green & red, Freight Rover Sherpa minibus 1790 (D790JUB) is seen here near Todmorden sporting a Yorkshire Rider Todmorden fleet name vinyl. *K.A.Jenkinson*

INTO EMPLOYEE OWNERSHIP

Another milestone was reached on 21 October 1988 when Yorkshire Rider was purchased by its employees under an Employee Share Ownership Plan in which free shares were issued to all the company's staff. In preparation for this move, the ESOP team registered a number of new companies the first of which was Simco No.243 Ltd. on 29 June which was later renamed (on 18 October) Rider Holdings Ltd. To mark the change in ownership of Yorkshire Rider, on 26 October (which was Launch Day), all buses were driven round for the whole of the day using dipped headlights; all staff wore a Yorkshire Rider 'Owner' lapel badge and a white carnation, and five buses which had been adorned with ESOP 3,500 Caring Owners logos operated in

To mark the purchase by its employees of Yorkshire Rider from the PTE, a bus in each of its operating districts was adorned with posters to indicate that the company was now in the hands of 3,500 caring owners. Halifax's example thus treated was lowheight NCME-bodied Leyland Olympian 5152 (F152XYG) which is seen here in Commercial Street on 26 October 1988. *K.A.Jenkinson*

For a few weeks in April 1989, Yorkshire Rider hired a number of former Bee Line Buzz Freight Rover Sherpa minibuses from dealers Carlyle of Birmingham. Still wearing its former owner's yellow & red livery but adorned with Yorkshire Rider Halifax fleet name vinyls, D258OOJ is seen at Ovenden whilst working circular service 520. *K.A.Jenkinson*

Repainted in the old Todmorden JOC livery of dark green & cream at the start of 1989, Plaxton-bodied Leyland Leopard 8534 (RWU534R) has retained these colours for almost ten years and is still painted thus. Seen outside Millwood depot, Todmorden in February 1989, it sported Yorkshire Rider Todmorden fleet names as well as the old Todmorden JOC logo. *K.A.Jenkinson*

On its final day in use on 22 April 1989, Crossfield bus station at Halifax plays host to an ex.GM Buses Fleetline, an indigenous NCME-bodied Fleetline and a Yorkshire Woollen District Transport ECW-bodied Bristol VRT. *K.A.Jenkinson*

On 22 April 1989, the last day of use of Crossfield bus station at Halifax, Yorkshire Rider Halifax's former GM Buses NCME-bodied Fleetline 7251 (BVR87T) was, ironically, about to depart on the 556 service to its old home city, Manchester.
K.A.Jenkinson

Leeds, Bradford, Halifax and Huddersfield carrying passengers free of charge.

Although 1989 was not to prove to be as eventful as the previous year, it was nevertheless one of expansion and one in which several new types of vehicle were examined for consideration of future orders. One of those which spent a day in Halifax was an Optare Delta-bodied DAF SB220 single deckers which was used in service between 14 and 16 February while a Carlyle-bodied Iveco minibus was also inspected. Further strangers in the town were a number of former Bee Line Buzz Freight Rover Sherpa minibuses which were hired from Birmingham-based dealer Carlyle for a few weeks commencing

18 March. Retaining their former owner's yellow and red livery to which Yorkshire Rider Halifax fleet names were added, these were used on services from the town centre to Ovenden before returning from whence they came towards the end of April. As far as service changes were concerned, under a new round of route tendering, at the end of February Yorkshire Rider took over the Halifax - Oldham section of service 556 (Halifax - Manchester) from Crosville Motor Services who, in turn, had gained it from Yelloways some three months earlier. Having eliminated one of its competitors from Halifax, on 2 June Yorkshire Rider took over three services previously operated by Ivy Coaches of Huddersfield, two of which (455 Hebden Bridge - Keighley and

New to West Yorkshire PTE for operation by Metro Calderdale, Plaxton-bodied Leyland Leopard 8515 (LUG515P) was one of two such vehicles transferred to Yorkshire Rider's West Yorkshire Road Car Co. subsidiary following its purchase of that company in August 1989. Repainted into West Yorkshire's red & cream livery, it retained these colours for a short while after rejoining the Halifax fleet early in the following year and is seen thus in Halifax bus station in April 1990 fitted with a Yorkshire Rider Limited vinyl rather than one carrying the Halifax district name.
K.A.Jenkinson

The last two ex.Halifax Corporation/JOC half-cab double deckers to survive into Yorkshire Rider days were Roe-bodied Leyland PD2/37s CCP164C and CCP523C, both of which ended their days as driver training buses. Seen here at Elmwood depot in April 1990, they had both recently been withdrawn from their duties and were awaiting disposal. *T.W.W.Knowles*

X37 Halifax - Huddersfield) involved Calderdale in their operation while on 21 June Rider purchased the local bus operations of Abbeyways who had competed on the Ovenden circular and Claremount services.

After an enormous amount of construction work had been carried out to ensure the preservation of the Sion Chapel and Sunday School, the new Halifax bus station was brought into use on 23 April 1989, replacing the Crossfield site which was closed without ceremony on the previous night. Although this accommodated most of Halifax's bus services, initially a number of cross-town routes continued to pick up passengers in the town centre and did not divert into the bus station until a later date.

In January 1990, of the new buses delivered to Yorkshire Rider, 5 of the 10 Plaxton Derwent-bodied Volvo B10Ms were allocated to Halifax where they quickly proved popular amongst passengers and staff alike. On the reverse side of the coin, however, August witnessed the demise of the last former Halifax/Calderdale JOC vehicle in the operational fleet when NCME-bodied Daimler Fleetline 3084 (RCP274K) was withdrawn from service. This still wore its PTE livery of Verona green and buttermilk, having never been repainted into Yorkshire Rider's colours due to its planned demise, although it was not the survivor in this scheme. Meanwhile, a large number of service changes were implemented in the Halifax area on 20 August in an attempt to effect economies without detriment to passengers while in April 1991 numerous timetable changes were made as a consequence of the PTA withdrawing financial support for early morning, evening and Sunday journeys.

After a period of comparative calm, on 23 February 1992 John Rigby Travel of Liversedge took over Yorkshire Rider Halifax service 588 (Portsmouth - Halifax General Hospital) while

following a new round of tendering, the PTE indicated its dissatisfaction with the bids submitted by Rider's Calderdale district by inviting Chesterfield Transport to tender for the services concerned. This, understandably, infuriated Yorkshire Rider who retaliated by threatening to challenge Chesterfield on its own territory if it proceeded, but in the event, although the Derbyshire-based undertaking was successful with its bids, due to some technicalities it was unable to take up its newly gained services which were then re-tendered and retained by Yorkshire Rider, thus averting another potential bus war. Later in the year, on 11 May the cross-town Bradford - Hubberton, Steep Lane and Boulderclough services (576/7/8) were split at Halifax, reverting to their original status as free standing routes while on 8 August Yorkshire Rider regained the 588 service from John Rigby Travel.

During the summer of 1993 Halifax received yet another new type of bus when it took delivery of 10 Alexander Strider-bodied Scania N113CRB single deckers, these displacing a similar number of double deck Fleetlines. At around this same time, on 21 June the 548 and 549 services from Halifax to Brighouse were converted to Flagship status using three of the new Scania single deckers and three of the newest Northern Counties-bodied Leyland Olympians. Flagship was the name given to a new passenger charter under which Yorkshire Rider made promises to provide vehicles of better standards of comfort and cleanliness together with the delivery of a reliable and punctual service with a specially selected team of drivers. This new status was extended to the 508 (Halifax - Leeds) and 576 (Halifax - Bradford via Queensbury) services on 31 January 1994, with all the buses used carrying small 'Flagship' boards in their windscreens, although on this occasion the vehicles used were not specially chosen and could be of any type within the Halifax fleet.

Freight Rover Sherpas 1862, 1865 and 1868 (D862/5/8LWR) take their Sunday rest at Skircoat Road depot in April 1995 together with a pair of former GM Buses Fleetlines and NCME-bodied Fleetline 7078. *K.A.Jenkinson*

TWO NEW OWNERS IN FIFTEEN MONTHS

Following almost five and a half years of employee ownership, surprisingly it was announced on 21 March 1994 that Weston-super-Mare based Badgerline Holdings plc had made a takeover bid for Rider Holdings and that the sale of the 51% shares held by Rider's management had already been agreed. Badgerline, however, required 75% of Rider's shares before it was able to proceed and after ballots had been held for the staff shareholders, it was confirmed on 14 April that Badgerline would take control four days later. Almost immediately, all Yorkshire Rider's vehicles received a white label in their rear window

the above events, however, one of Todmorden depot's Northern Counties-bodied Leyland Olympians was repainted into the old Todmorden JOC livery of dark green and cream as part of Yorkshire Rider's 'Building on a Great Tradition' fleet in which the liveries of all the constituent companies were represented, while six months later a dual-purpose Plaxton-bodied Leyland Tigers (1606) was unexpectedly repainted into the cream, orange and green colours of the erstwhile Halifax undertaking.

Having been largely free from competition in the Halifax area from other operators, Yorkshire Rider suddenly found itself facing

The first of Yorkshire Rider Halifax's new NCME-bodied Volvo Olympians, 5301 (L301PWR), was painted in Flagship colours and used almost exclusively on the services to Bradford and Brighouse. On this occasion, it was working a 576 journey to Bradford and was caught by the camera starting the steep climb from Boothtown to Queensbury. *K.A.Jenkinson*

depicting the Badger logo and incorporating the wording 'A Badgerline Company' and the deed was done. Almost before the ink had dried on the takeover documents, Halifax received 5 new single deckers in the form of Alexander Strider-bodied Volvo B10Bs, these replacing the Scanias acquired during the previous year. Joining these at the start of June were 15 new Northern Counties-bodied Volvo Olympian double deckers, one of which was painted in Flagship colours, and amongst the vehicles withdrawn as a consequence, 5 of former GM Buses Fleetlines which were, surprisingly, sold back to their original owner. Prior to

a challenge from newcomer T.J.Walsh who began operating minibuses on a mornings only circular service from Halifax to Ovenden Way on 20 June 1994. Seeing this as a threat to its own services in the Ovenden area, Yorkshire Rider introduced an identical service (numbered 825) on 11 July, running two minutes ahead of its competitor. Far from being deterred by this action, T.J.Walsh started another service on 19 September from Halifax to Siddal, this running only in the afternoons and on 28 November, a second mornings only service to Ovenden Way was inaugurated.

Looking immaculate in the dark green & cream livery of the erstwhile Todmorden JOC, Yorkshire Rider's lowheight NCME-bodied Leyland Olympian 5156 (F156XYG) seen here at Halifax bus station was thus painted as a member of Rider's 'Building on a Great Tradition' fleet.

Director and senior management team and these were put into operation on 1 September. Under this reorganisation, a new subsidiary was formed under the title of CalderLine to take over Halifax and Todmorden depots which together had a fleet of 172 vehicles (167 operational, 2 driver trainers and 3 delicensed) and as a consequence the legal lettering on all the above was changed to 'Yorkshire Rider Ltd. t/a CalderLine'. Although at first the existing Rider livery of green and cream was retained, this was modified to incorporate more green on the lower panels on which to accommodate the new fleet name.

Before the year ended, in a bid to upgrade its minibus fleet in Halifax, Yorkshire Rider at the start of December placed in service 6 new Plaxton Beaver-bodied Mercedes Benz 709D minibuses, the first two of which were painted in an unrelieved white livery while the remainder wore Flagship colours for use on the recently upgraded 830-3 group of services.

Having spent less than a year under Badgerline ownership, following the latter's merger with Aberdeen-based GRT Holdings under the new title of FirstBus, on 16 June 1995 Yorkshire Rider became a subsidiary of the new group. This resulted in the immediate replacement of the Badgerline vinyls in the rear window of all Rider's buses with a new FirstBus logo which was also placed in the front window adjacent to the passenger entrance, although on the horizon were more dramatic changes. Prior to the merger of Badgerline and GRT Holdings, plans had been drawn up for the division of Yorkshire Rider into a number of separate operating companies, each with its own Managing

In the meantime. T.J.Walsh, whose fleet had now grown to 11 minibuses, had further expanded with the introduction of two more new services, one from Halifax to Illingworth on 23 October 1995 and the other from Halifax to Elland on 7 November, both of which competed with established services of CalderLine. A further threat, this time by Yorkshire Blue Bus who began operations on the 576 service between Halifax and Bradford on 5 March 1996, soon disappeared, however, when unbelievably it was withdrawn after only five days.

More new Plaxton Beaver-bodied Mercedes Benz 709D minibuses were received arrived during the first few months of 1996, replacing all but two of the Freight Rover Sherpas while more surprising was the repurchase on 6 December of one of the GM Buses NCME-bodied Fleetlines which had originally crossed the Pennines to join Yorkshire Rider at Halifax in 1987 and was resold to GM Buses North in 1994. Equally unexpected was the return to service in June of a former Halifax JOC 1950 vintage Park Royal-bodied AEC Regent III which had been privately preserved since 1969. Owned by new independent operator Halifax Joint Committee and retaining its original orange, green and cream livery, it was put to work for the duration of the summer on a heritage service between Halifax and Hebden Bridge and was also used on evening Countryside Tours on Saturdays and Sundays. The success of this operation was such that it recommenced at the start of the 1997 summer season and in October of that year a second service was started from Huddersfield to Hebden Bridge with positioning journeys between Halifax and Huddersfield. To supplement the AEC Regent III, a trio of former London Buses Routemasters were purchased in the autumn of 1997 by Halifax Joint Committee and were painted in various styles of Halifax's erstwhile livery as a superb reminder of the past.

In April 1996, CalderLine's image was changed yet again when a new livery of white with a blue skirt and yellow band, both of which were upswept at the rear, was adopted along with a corporate FirstBus-style fleet name and 'F' logo. Although the new colour scheme was applied only to the newer members of the fleet, several buses still painted in the old Yorkshire Rider green and cream scheme were given the corporate-style fleet name and thus once more Halifax became a town of differing colours within the same fleet. Concurrent with these changes, CalderLine supplemented its fleet with a further 3 NCME-bodied Fleetlines which it acquired from First Manchester and were initially operated in their former owner's colours or a combination of these and CalderLine livery

Although the number of service changes implemented during 1997 were fewer than in previous years, a new limited stop route was started on 14 April branded 'Swiftlink'. Maintained jointly with FirstBus subsidiary Kingfisher Huddersfield, this was designed to reduce congestion in both towns by encouraging commuters to leave their cars at home and use the bus. For operation on this new X36 service, Swiftlink branding was added to the sides of five CalderLine vehicles (2 Alexander-bodied Volvo B10Bs, 2 Plaxton Paramount-bodied Leyland Tigers and a Duple Dominant bus-bodied Leyland Tiger) as well as to a number of Kingfisher's Plaxton Verde-bodied Dennis Lances.

Despite having taken the decision not to introduce a nationwide corporate livery, FirstGroup (as FirstBus was renamed during the final month of 1997) did a partial U-turn by announcing that a new colour scheme of white with blue and magenta relief was to be introduced for all its subsidiaries' new buses which incorporated the Group's new standard interior, although those which did not comply would continue to be operated in their existing colours. Additionally, all the existing fleet names were to be replaced by a new 'First' identity with the operating company's name applied in lettering of a reduced size, and thus CalderLine was to undergo yet another visual change as far as its buses were concerned.

1998 began with the announcement that CalderLine was to receive a substantial number of new buses during the year including some Alexander Royale-bodied Volvo Olympian double deckers, low-floor Plaxton Pointer-bodied Dennis Dart SLFs, and Plaxton Beaver-bodied Mercedes Benz Vario minibuses, all except the latter painted in the new FirstGroup corporate colours of white, magenta and blue, thus introducing a third livery to the CalderLine fleet. Amongst the vehicles these would replace were, surprisingly, a number of the 1994 Northern Counties-bodied Volvo Olympians which were to be transferred to Essex Buses for use in its Eastern National fleet rather than the ex.GM Buses Fleetlines which were apparently to be left to soldier on into the future! Before any of the new corporate liveried double or single deckers were received, however, 4 new Plaxton Beaver-bodied Mercedes Benz Vario minibuses were diverted from Eastern National and were placed in service in Halifax wearing that company's green and yellow livery to provide the town with yet more different colours. Almost unbelievably, yet another new livery made its appearance in Halifax on 23 March when a new express service to Leeds via Brighouse using the M62 motorway for a large part of its journey was inaugurated jointly with First Leeds. For its operation, CalderLine acquired an Alexander Strider-bodied Scania N113CRB single decker from First Leeds and painted it in a dedicated livery of white and blue. Soon afterwards, the first of the company's new buses arrived, these being Plaxton Pointer-bodied Dennis Darts which in addition to being the first to wear FirstGroup's new corporate livery were also the first of low-floor specification. Initially used on the Illingworth group of services, these carried route details on their cove panels, although this lettering was removed during September to enable their use on other services as well. Following soon afterwards, the new Volvo Olympians, numbering 10, began to arrive and were put in service on the 508 (Halifax - Leeds) and 576 (Halifax - Bradford) routes during May while in August delivery of the Plaxton Beaver-bodied Mercedes Benz Vario minibuses commenced and enabled those diverted from Eastern National earlier in the year (which had manual gearboxes) to be withdrawn and disposed of to another FirstGroup company. In

view of the fact that the new Varios were not fitted with FirstGroup standard interiors, they were painted in the revised white, blue and yellow CalderLine livery which omitted the rear upsweep of the yellow and blue and had been introduced a few weeks earlier.

Meanwhile, local independent Halifax Joint Committee withdrew most of its journeys on its Huddersfield - Hebden Bridge service with effect from 13 July and instead began operations between Halifax and Sowerby and at weekends between Hebden Bridge, Shelf and Bradford, all of which competed with First CalderLine. Whilst the majority of these proved highly successful, the Shelf service was soon withdrawn and later, on 28 September, reduced weekend operations were introduced for the duration of the winter.

To mark the centenary of passenger transport in Halifax, a special bus service was operated by First CalderLine on 28 June from Westgate to Wainhouse Tower at King Cross using two of the recently delivered new low-floor Dennis Darts. Although the service, which operated every ten minutes, was free, passengers had to purchase a commemorative souvenir ticket for 1p (1d being the original fare charged in 1898).

Finally, in October 1998 First Calderline introduced new Gold Service standards to four of its routes (508 Halifax - Leeds; 543 Highroad Well - Siddal; 544 Highroad Well - Southowram and 576 Halifax - Bradford), the charter for which offered passengers high quality vehicles (the Alexander Royale-bodied Volvo Olympians and low-floor Plaxton Pointer-bodied Dennis Dart SLFs), specially trained drivers, cleaner buses and better service reliability in a similar fashion to the Flagship service which had quietly been discontinued at an earlier date.

Despite in its true sense municipal transport in Halifax only enjoyed a life of some 76 years, together with its successors West Yorkshire PTE, Yorkshire Rider and First CalderLine, it has now reached its centenary and the town now looks forward to entering the millennium in the same way that it entered the twentieth century, providing an efficient daily public transport service for its residents and those of its surrounding areas. Although the trams and trolleybuses are now nothing more than a memory, happily the orange, green and cream livery which had for so long been an integral part of the townscape still survives,

even though it is now confined to the four independently owned buses of Halifax Joint Committee, proving that some things, at least, have not disappeared completely.

ROUTES

HALIFAX BUS ROUTES FOLLOWING THE CLOSURE OF THE TRAMWAY SYSTEM ON 14 FEBRUARY 1939

HALIFAX CORPORATION

17 Halifax (Commercial Street) - Nursery Lane (Vegal Crescent) via Bank Top and Ovenden Road.
18 Halifax (Commercial Street) - Beechwood Road via Bank Top, Ovenden Road and Keighley Road.
19 Halifax (Commercial Street) - Raw Lane (Illingworth) via Bank Top, Ovenden Road and Keighley Road.
20 Halifax (Commercial Street) - Causeway Foot via Bank Top, Ovenden Road and Keighley Road.
21 Halifax (Cow Green) - Wainstalls via Pellon Lane and Moor End Road.
21A Halifax (Cow Green) - Mount Tabor via Pellon Lane and Moor End Road.
22 Halifax (Cow Green) - Raw Lane (Illingworth) via Pellon Lane, Moor End Road, Mill Lane and Mixenden Road.
23 Halifax (Wards End) - Salterhebble (Jubilee Road) via Bailey Hall Road, Siddal New Road, Oxford Lane and Jubilee Road.
23A Salterhebble (Jubilee Road) - Washer Lane *(Circular)* via Siddal new Road, Bailey Hall Road, Alexandra Street, Trinity Road, Savile Park Road, The Moor, Scarr Bottom, Washer Lane, Pye Nest Road, King Cross and Haugh Shaw Road .
23B Washer Lane - Salterhebble (Jubilee Road) *(Circular)* via Haugh Shaw Road, King Cross, Pye Nest Road, Washer Lane, Scarr Bottom, The Moor, Savile Park Road, Trinity Road, Alexandra Street, Bailey Hall Road and Siddal New Road.
24 Halifax (Albion Street) - Wheatley via Lee Bridge, Shroggs Road, Wheatley Road (or City Lane, Long Lane and Scar Head) and Crag Lane.
24A Halifax (Albion Street) - Nursery Lane (Vegal Crescent) via Lee Bridge, Shroggs Lane, City Lane, Long Lane, Scar Head and Denfield Lane.
25 Halifax (Southgate) - Inner Circle (Queens Road) via Fountain Street, West Parade, Parkinson Lane, Queens Road, Hanson Lane and Pellon Lane (in both directions).
26 Halifax (Albion Street) - Bradshaw (Pit Hill) via Lee Bridge, Ovenden Road, Shay Lane, Holdsworth Road, Riley Lane and Bradshaw Lane.
27 Copley - Warley or Newlands via Copley Lane, Skircoat Green Road, Heath Road, Skircoat Road, Wards End/Alexandra Street, Bull Green, Hopwood Lane, Warley Road, Highroad Well and Stock Lane.
28 Halifax (Cow Green) - Norton Tower (Royles Head) via Pellon Lane, Hanson Lane, Albert Road and Highroad Well Lane.
29 Halifax (Powell Street) - Outer Circle (West End) via Pellon Lane, Springhall Road, West End, Warley Road, King Cross, Savile Park, Free School Lane and Skircoat Road. (In opposite direction from Halifax Arcade Royal).
29A Halifax (Powell Street) - Sandbeds *(Circular)* via Pellon Lane, Pellon New Road, Sandbeds Road, Albert Road, Spring Hall Lane and Pellon Lane (in both directions).
30 Halifax (Westgate) - Southowram (Towngate) via New Bank Road, Beacon Hill Road, Bank Top and Pinnar Lane.
31 West End - General Hospital (Godfrey Road) *(Circular)* via Spring Hall Lane, Gibbet Street, Westholme Road, Hopwood Lane, Commercial Street, Skircoat Road, Heath Road and Skircoat Green Road.
31 West End - General Hospital (Godfrey Road) *(Circular)* via Warley Road, King Cross Lane, Commercial Street, Skircoat Road, Heath Road and Skircoat Green Road.
32 Halifax (Westgate) - Northowram (Queen Victoria Inn) via New Bank, Godley Lane, Stump Cross and Bradford Road.
33 Halifax (Westgate) - Shibden ((Merry Boys Inn) via New Bank, Godley Lane, Stump Cross, Kell Lane, Brow Lane and Blake Hill End.
34 Halifax (Union Street) - Boothtown via Haley Hill and Boothtown Road.
34A Halifax (Union Street) - Boothtown via New Bank, Horley Green and Claremount Road.
35 Halifax (Alexandra Street) - Salterhebble (Punch Bowl Inn) via Skircoat Road, Huddersfield Road and Salterhebble Hill.
35A Halifax (Commercial Street) - Highroad Well (Sandhall Lane) via Gibbet Street.
36 Halifax (Old Station) - Bairstow Lane *(Circular)* via Horton Street, King Cross Road, King Cross, Burnley Road, Cote Hill, Bairstow Lane, Willow Hall Lane, Rochdale Road, King Cross, King Cross Lane and Horton Street (in both directions).
36A Halifax (Old Station) - Tuel Lane via Horton Street, King Cross Road, King Cross, Burnley Road and Cote Hill.

HALIFAX JOINT OMNIBUS COMMITTEE

41 Elland (Catherine Street) - Triangle via Elland Bridge, Elland Wood Bottom, Wakefield Road and Sowerby Bridge.
42 Halifax (Powell Street) - White Hart via King Cross, Rochdale Road, Bolton Brow, Sowerby Bridge and Ripponden.
43 Halifax (King Edward Street) - Huddersfield (Springwood Street) via Skircoat Road, Huddersfield Road, Elland Wood Bottom, Elland Bridge, Elland and The Ainleys.
43B Ripponden (Elland Road) - Elland (Catherine Street) via Barkisland, Saddleworth Road, West Vale and Long Wall.
44 Halifax (Powell Street) - Steep Lane via King Cross, Pye Nest Road, Sowerby Bridge, Sowerby New Road, Sowerby and Rooley Lane.
45 Halifax (King Edward Street) - Beech Road (Sowerby Bridge) via West Parade, King Cross, Rochdale Road and Park Road.
45A Halifax (Powell Street) - Sowerby Bridge (Station Road) via King Cross and Pye Nest Road.
46 Halifax (Alexandra Street) - Heptonstall via King Cross, Burnley Road, Tuel Lane, Luddenden Foot, Mytholmroyd, Hebden Bridge, Mytholm and Heptonstall Slack.
46A Halifax (Powell Street) - Hebden Bridge via King Cross, Burnley Road, Tuel Lane, Luddenden Foot and Mytholmroyd.
47 Halifax (Alexandra Street) - Midgley via King Cross, Burnley Road, Luddenden Foot, Luddenden Lane and Solomon Hill.
48 Halifax (Carrier Street) - Brighouse (Thornton Square) via New Bank, Stump Cross, Hipperholme, Hove Edge and Slead Syke.
49 Halifax (Carrier Street) - Brighouse (Thornton Square) via New Bank, Stump Cross, Hipperholme, Hove Edge and Bonegate.
50 Halifax (Carrier Street) - Brighouse (Thornton Square) via Beach Hill Road, Bank Top, Church Lane, Delvers and Brookfoot.
51 Halifax (Alexandra Street) - West Vale (Stainland Road) via Skircoat Road, Huddersfield Road, Salterhebble and Stainland Road.
51A Halifax (Alexandra Street) - Stainland (Black Horse) via Skircoat Road, Huddersfield Road, Salterhebble, Stainland Road and Holywell Green.
51B Halifax (Alexandra Street) - Outlane via Skircoat Road, Huddersfield Road, Salterhebble, Stainland Road, Holywell Green, Stainland, Stainland Road or Park Lane and Forest Hill Lane.
52 Halifax (Powell Street) - Rishworth via King Cross, Rochdale Road, Sowerby Bridge, Triangle and Ripponden.
52A Halifax (Powell Street) - Cunning Corner via King Cross, Rochdale Road, Sowerby Bridge, Triangle, Ripponden and Rishworth.
52B Halifax (Powell Street) - Commons via King Cross, Rochdale Road, Sowerby Bridge, Triangle, Ripponden and Rishworth.
53 Cragg Vale - Hebden Bridge via Crag Road, Mytholmroyd and Burnley Road.
53A Beechwood (St.Peters Avenue) - Albert Road *(Circular)* via Providence, Sowerby New Road, Sowerby Bridge, Beech Road, Tuel Lane and Albert Road.
54 Halifax (King Edward Street) - Hullenedge (Harmerstones Road) via Skircoat Road, Huddersfield Road, Salterhebble, Stainland Road, West Vale, Long Wall and Victoria Road.
54A Halifax (King Edward Street) - Blackley via Skircoat Road, Huddersfield Road, Salterhebble, Stainland Road, West Vale, Long Wall, Victoria Road, Hammerstones Road and Blackley Road.
55 Halifax (King Edward Street) - Greetland (Turbury Lane) via Skircoat Road, Huddersfield Road, Salterhebble, Stainland Road, West Vale, Rochdale Road and Cross Hills.
55A Halifax (King Edward Street) - Barkisland via Skircoat Road, Huddersfield Road, Salterhebble, Stainland Road, West Vale, Rochdale Road, Crosshills and Greetland Road.
56 Halifax (King Edward Street) - Norland (Moorcock) via Skircoat Road, Huddersfield Road, Salterhebble, Stainland Road, West Vale, Rochdale Road, Cross Hills, Turbury Lane and Shaw Lane.
57 Elland (Catherine Street) - Outlane via Savile Road, Victoria Road, Broad Carr, Holywell Brook, Holywell Green, Stainland, Stainland Road or Park Lane and Forest Hill Road.
58 Elland (Catherine Street) - Norland (Moorcock) via Long Wall, West Vale, Rochdale Road, Crosshills, Spring Rock and Shaw Lane.
59 Halifax (Union Street) - Queensbury (Cenotaph) via Haley Hill, Boothtown, Catherine Slack, Ambler Thorn and Ford Hill.
60 Halifax (King Edward Street) - Mill Bank via King Cross, Rochdale Road, Sowerby Bridge, Triangle, Oak Hill and Cottonstones.
61 Ripponden - Sowerby Bridge (Wharf Street) via Rochdale Road, Redon, Mill Bank and Triangle.

HALIFAX CORPORATION

Fleet No.	Reg'n No.	Chassis	Body	Notes
1912				
1	CP272	Daimler CC	Commercial Car Hirers B28C	
1913				
2	CP281	Daimler CC	Commercial Car Hirers B28C	
3	CP284	Daimler CC	Commercial Car Hirers B28C	
1916				
4	CP742	Daimler Y	Halifax Corporation B23R	
5-6	CP747-8	Daimler Y	Halifax Corporation B23R	
1918				
103-4	-----	Railless	Milnes Voss B28R	**Trolleybuses** Ex.Dundee Corporation. Registered CP2020/1 in 1921
1921				
6	CP93	AEC YC	Halifax Corporation B24F	Originally a tower wagon new in 1919
1922				
7	CP2418	Dennis 50-cwt	Halifax Corporation B24F	
1923				
8	CP3037	Dennis 50-cwt	Halifax Corporation B24F	
1924				
2	CP3457	Tilling Stevens RC2	Halifax Corporation B26F	**Trolleybus**
1925				
9-14	CP3810-5	Dennis 50-cwt	Strachan & Brown B26F	
15-6	CP3905-6	Dennis 50-cwt	Halifax Corporation B26F	
17-20	CP4397-400	Dennis 50-cwt	Halifax Corporation B26F	
1926				
21-3	CP4987-9	Dennis 50-cwt	Strachan & Brown B26F	To JOC 1929
24-9	CP5226-31	Karrier CL4	Hall Lewis B26F	
1927				
1-6	CP5734-9	Karrier CL6	Hall Lewis B26F	To JOC 1929
31/3-6	CP6221/3-6	Karrier CL6	Hall Lewis B26F	To JOC 1929
30	CX8989	Karrier CY6	Hall Lewis B25F	Ex.Karrier Motors demonstrator new 1926. To JOC 1929
37	CP5850	Karrier CL4	Hall Lewis B26F	Ex.Ryburn Garage new 1927. To JOC 1929
38	CP5749	Karrier CL4	Hall Lweis B26F	Ex.Ryburn Garage new 1926. To JOC 1929
39	CP5123	Karrier CL4	Hall Lewis B26F	Ex.Ryburn Garage new 1927. To JOC 1929
40	CP5478	Karrier CL4	Hall Lewis B26F	Ex.Ryburn Garage new 1926. To JOC 1929
41	CP4722	Karrier JK	?	Ex.Ryburn Garage new 1926. To JOC 1929
42	CX8039	Karrier JK	?	
1928				
32	CP6222	Karrier CL6	Hall Lewis B26F	To JOC 1929
49	CP6692	Karrier Z	Halifax Corporation B14F	
43-8	CP6925-30	Karrier WL6	Harris & Hassall B32D	To JOC 1929
1929				
50	CP8006	Karrier JKL	Hall Lewis B32R	
52	CP8008	Leyland TS2	Leyland B31R	
53-5	CP8009-11	AEC Regent	Short H26/24RO	
1930				
51	CP8007	Dennis EV	English Electric B31D	
56	CP8167	AEC Regent	Short H26/24RO	
57	MT2114	AEC Regent	Short H26/24RO	Ex.AEC demonstrator new 1929
1931				
58	CP9061	AEC Regent	Short H26/24RO	
107-15	CP9070-8	AEC Regent	Hoyal H26/24RO	
121-3	CP9447-49	AEC Regal	English Electric B32R	
1932				
116-20	CP9442-6	AEC Regent	English Electric H26/24RO	
124	CP9450	AEC Regal	English Electric B32R	
1933				
2-6	JX321-5	AEC Regent	English Electric H26/24RO	
1934				
7	JX1461	AEC Q	English Electric H59F	
10-1	JX1788/90	AEC Regent	Park Royal H26/26R	
12-3	JX1912-3	AEC Regent	Roe H25/26R	
14-5	JX2037-8	AEC Regent	English Electric H30/26R	
1935				
8	AMV482	AEC Regent	Park Royal H30/26R	Ex.AEC demonstrator new 1934
9	MV3522	AEC Regent	Park Royal H28/26R	Ex.AEC demonstrator new 1932
16-23	JX2301-8	AEC Regent	Roberts H24/24R	
24	CML516	AEC Regent	Park Royal H30/26R	Ex.AEC demonstrator new 1935
25-7	JX3420-2	AEC Regal	Park Royal B32R	
28-30	JX3423-5	AEC Regal	Roe B32R	
1937				
31-4	JX5261-4	AEC Regent	Park Royal H30/26R	
1938				
35-7	JX6162-3	AEC Regent	Park Royal H30/26R	
38	JX6424	AEC Regent	Park Royal H30/26R	
39	JX6265	AEC Regent	Park Royal H30/26R	
40-2	JX6425-7	AEC Regent	Park Royal H30/26R	
43	JX6264	AEC Regent	Park Royal H30/26R	
44-5	JX6428-9	AEC Regent	Park Royal H30/26R	
46	JX6266	AEC Regent	Park Royal H30/26R	
47-9	JX6568-70	AEC Regent	Roe H31/25R	
50-2/7	JX6557-60	AEC Regal	Park Royal B32R	
59-65	JX6892-8	AEC Regent	Roe H31/25R	
68	JX6901	AEC Regent	Roe H31/25R	
72-9	JX6928-35	AEC Regent	Park Royal H30/26R	

Fleet No.	Reg'n No.	Chassis	Body	Notes
1939				
53-6	JX7050-3	AEC Regent	Park Royal H30/26R	
58	JX7058	AEC Regent	Roe H31/25R	
66-7	JX6899-900	AEC Regent	Roe H31/25R	
69-70	JX6902-3	AEC Regent	Roe H31/25R	
71	JX7059	AEC Regent	Roe H31/25R	
80-3	JX7046-9	AEC Regent	Park Royal H30/26R	81 converted to recovery wagon 1952
84-7	JX7054-7	AEC Regent	Weymann H30/26R	
1940				
88	JX8106	AEC Regent	Park Royal H30.26R	
1946				
301-8	JX9401-8	AEC Regent IIIRT	Roe H31/25R	305-8 to JOC 1947. Back to Corporation 1954
1947				
309-17	ACP414-22	AEC Regent III	Park Royal H30/26R	
335-41	ACP384-90	Leyland PD2/1	Leyland H30/26R	335 to driver trainer 1959
1948				
305-8	ACP631-4	AEC Regent III	Roe H31/25R	
318-21	ACP423-6	AEC Regent III	Park Royal H30/26R	
322-5	ACP800-3	AEC Regent III	Park Royal H30/26R	
326-34	ACP915-23	AEC Regent III	Park Royal H30/26R	331 to JOC 1965
342-3	ACP391-2	Leyland PD2/1	Leyland H30/26R	342 to driver trainer 1963. 343 to JOC 1965
1949				
344-6	BCP533-5	AEC Regal III	Roe B32R	
347-8	BCP536-7	AEC Regent III	Roe H31/25R	
1951				
349-54	CCP601-6	Daimler CD650	East Lancs H30/26R	
355-59	CCP607-11	AEC Regent III	Park Royal H30/26R	
1952				
360	CCP612	AEC Regent III	Park Royal H30/26R	
1954				
87-98	DCP831-42	Daimler CVG6	Roe H33/25R	95/6 to JOC 1968, 97/8 to JOC 1967
1956				
15-9	GJX327-31	Daimler CVG6	Roe H37/28R	15-9 to JOC 1971 then to CJOC 1971. 19 to WYPTE 1974
1958				
1-9	KCP1-9	Leyland RT3/1	Weymann B42F	1-4 to CJOC 1972, 5-9 to CJOC 1974. 1-9 to WYPTE 1974
1960				
11-8	LJX11-8	AEC Regent V	MCCW H40/32F	11-3/5-7 to JOC 1970 and 11/12 to CJOC 1971
21-8	MJX21-8	Leyland PD2/37	MCCW H36/28F	To WYPTE 1974
1962				
31-9	PJX31-9	Leyland L1	Weymann B42F	37-9 to JOC 1971 then to CJOC 1971. 37 back to Corporation 1974. 31-9 to WYPTE 1974
41-8	PJX41-8	Leyland PD2/37	Weymann H36/28F	41-2 to JOC 1971 then to CJOC 1971. 41-8 to WYPTE 1974
1964				
40	LUA440	AEC Regent III	Roe H31/25R	Ex.Leeds City Transport new 1948. To JOC 1965
49	LUA427	AEC Regent III	Roe H31/25R	Ex.Leeds City Transport new 1947
51/6/7	TCP51/6/7	Leyland PD3/4	Weymann H40/32F	To WYPTE 1974
1965				
19-20	TWJ505-6	AEC Monocoach	Park Royal B44F	Ex.Sheffield JOC new 1955. To JOC 1967
52-5/8	TCP51-5/8	Leyland PD3/4	Weymann H40/32F	To WYPTE 1974
59-66	CCP159-66C	Leyland PD2/37	Roe H37/28F	To WYPTE 1974
1966				
67-74	DCP67-74D	Leyland PD2/37	Weymann H36/28F	To WYPTE 1974
99-105	ECP679-85D	Daimler CRG6LX	NCME H43/32F	103 to JOC 1971 then to CJOC 1971. 99-105 to WYPTE 1974
1967				
97-8	GJX317-8F	Daimler CRG6LX	NCME H43/31F	To WYPTE 1974
106-8	FJX506-8E	Daimler SRG6LX	Willowbrook B45F	To WYPTE 1974
1968				
95-6	JJX595-6G	Daimler CRG6LX	NCME H43/32F	To WYPTE 1974
111	JJX371G	Daimler SRG6LX	Willowbrook B45F	To WYPTE 1974
403	MKH81	Leyland PD2/12	Roe FCH30/20RD	Ex.East Yorkshire new 1952. Driver trainer
1969				
109-10	KCP379-80G	Daimler SRG6LX	Pennine B45F	To WYPTE 1974
112-4	KCP422-4G	Daimler SRG6LX	Willowbrook B45F	To WYPTE 1974
1970				
87	MJX14J	Daimler CRG6LX	NCME H43/31F	To WYPTE 1974
88-93	MJX8-13J	Daimler CRG6LX	NCME H43/31F	To WYPTE 1974
94	LJX404H	Daimler CRG6LX	NCME H43/31F	To WYPTE 1974
1971				
75	NCP475	AEC Regent V	MCCW H39/32F	Ex.Hebble new 1960. To CJOC 1972
76	RCP237	AEC Regent V	NCME H39/32F	Ex.Hebble new 1962. To CJOC 1972. To WYPTE 1974
103	BHD222C	Daimler CRG6LX	Alexander H44/31F	Ex.Yorkshire Woollen new 1966. To WYPTE 1974
123-4	PCP803-4	AEC Reliance	Alexander B43F	Ex.Hebble new 1962. 123 to WYPTE 1974
1972				
1-5	SCP341-5L	Leyland PSU4B/2R	Plaxton B45F	To WYPTE 1974
82-6	RCP272-6K	Daimler CRG6LX	NCME H43/31F	To WYPTE 1974
1973				
6-10	UJX916-20M	Leyland PSU4B/2R	Plaxton B45F	To WYPTE 1974

HALIFAX JOINT OMNIBUS COMMITTEE

Fleet No.	Reg'n No.	Chassis	Body	Notes
1929				
70-1	CP3750-1	Leyland SG9	Leyland B38F	Ex.Hebble new 1924
72	CP4692	Albion PJ26	Knape B26F	Ex.Hebble new 1926
73	CP5295	Albion PJ26	Knape B26F	Ex.Hebble new 1926
74	CP5610	Karrier KL	Karrier B35F	Ex.Hebble new 1927
75	CP5970	Albion PM28	Massey B32F	Ex.Hebble new 1927
76-7	CP5968-9	Albion PM28	Massey B32F	Ex.Hebble new 1927
78	CP6096	Karrier CL6	Davidson B32F	Ex.Hebble new 1927

79-80	CP6762-3	Albion PM28	? B32F	Ex.Hebble new 1928
81-2	CP6766-7	Albion PM28	? B32F	Ex.Hebble new 1928
83-4	CH7903/9	Leyland PLSC3	LMSR B32R	Ex.LMS Railway Co. new 1929
1930				
60	WU5818	Gotfredson	? B16F	Ex.G.Garrad new 1926
61	WU3768	Gotfredson	? B16F	Ex.G.Garrad new 1925
62	WW596	Albion PJ26	? B26	Ex.G.Garrad new 1927
63	WW6847	Albion PM28	? B32	Ex.G.Garrad new 1928
64	WW7526	Albion PM28	? B32	Ex.G.Garrad new 1928
65	YX3450	Gilford	? C24	Ex.G.Garrad new 1929
66	CP8168	AEC Regent	Short H26/24RO	
67-9	CP8646-8	AEC Regent	Short H26/24RO	
1931				
85-6	CP9062-3	AEC Regent	Hoyal H26/24RO	
87-9	CP9079-81	AEC Regent	Hoyal H26/24RO	
91-4	CP9064-7	AEC Regal	English Electric B32R	
95-6	CP9068-9	AEC Regent	Hoyal H26/24RO	
97-8	CP9440-1	AEC Regal	English Electric B32R	
1932				
90	CP9439	AEC Regent	Hoyal H28/24RO	
99-102	JX42-5	AEC Regal	English Electric B32R	
103-5	JX46-8	AEC Regent	English Electric H26/24RO	
125	WX7668	AEC Regal 4	Burlingham C32R	Ex.C.Avison new 1931
131-2	JX59-50	AEC Ranger	English Electric B20F	
1933				
126-30	JX326-30	AEC Regal	English Electric B32R	
133-6	JX331-4	AEC Regent	English Electric H26/24RO	
1934				
106	YG4626	Commer Centurion	? B20F	Ex.J.W.Halstead new 1933
137-8	JX1787/9	AEC Regent	Park Royal H26/26R	
139-40	JX2039-40	AEC Regent	English Electric H30/24R	
141-2	JX1914-5	AEC Regent	Roe H25/26R	
143-4	JX1954-5	AEC Regal	Park Royal B32R	
145-6	JX2106-7	AEC Regal	English Electric B32R	
147	YG710	Leyland TD2	Leyland L27/24R	Ex.Ripponden & District new 1932
148	YG3715	Leyland TD2	Leyland L27/24R	Ex.Ripponden & District new 1933
149	WX2073	AEC Reliance	Taylor B32F	Ex.Ripponden & District new 1929
150/1	WX3258/60	Leyland TS2	Leyland B30F	Ex.Ripponden & District new 1930
152-5	JX2297-300	AEC Regent	Roberts H28/26R	
1935				
-	HL2927	Leyland LSC1	Leyland B31F	Ex.Walton & Helliwell new 1926
156	YG3959	Commer Centaur	? B20F	Ex.Walton & Helliwell new 1933
157	JX3426	AEC Regal	Roe B32R	
158	JX3427	AEC Regal	Park Royal B32R	
1936				
159	JX3428	AEC Regal	Park Royal B32R	
160	JX3726	AEC Regent	Park Royal H30/26R	
161	JX3731	AEC Regent	Park Royal H30/26R	
162	JX3730	AEC Regent	Park Royal H30/26R	
163	JX3729	AEC Regent	Park Royal H30/26R	
164	JX3727	AEC Regent	Park Royal H30/26R	
165	JX3733	AEC Regent	Park Royal H30/26R	
166	JX3732	AEC Regent	Park Royal H30/26R	
167	JX3728	AEC Regent	Park Royal H30/26R	
168-9	JX3735-6	AEC Regent	Park Royal H30/26R	
170	JX3734	AEC Regent	Park Royal H30/26R	
171	JX3737	AEC Regent	Park Royal H30/26R	
-	WX8406	Bedford WLG	? B20F	Ex.F.A.Sutcliffe new 1931. Not operated.
1937				
172-9	JX5265-72	AEC Regent	Park Royal H30/26R	
1938				
181	JX6571	AEC Regent	Roe H31/25R	
182	JX6575	AEC Regent	Roe H31/25R	
183	JX6572	AEC Regent	Roe H31/25R	
184	JX6576	AEC Regent	Roe H31/25R	
185	JX6573	AEC Regent	Roe H31/25R	
186-7	JX6577-8	AEC Regent	Roe H31/25R	
188	JX6561	AEC Regal	Roe B32R	
189	JX6579	AEC Regal	Roe B32R	
190	JX6582	AEC Regal	Roe B32R	
191	JX6580	AEC Regal	Roe B32R	
192	JX6583	AEC Regal	Roe B32R	
193	JX6581	AEC Regal	Roe B32R	
194	JX6584	AEC Regal	Roe B32R	
1939				
195-7	JX7701-3	AEC Regal	Park Royal B32R	
198-9	JX7704-5	Leyland KPZO3	Park Royal B20F	
200	JX6939	AEC Regent	Park Royal H30/26R	
201-3	JX6936-8	AEC Regent	Park Royal H30/26R	
204-8	JX7706-10	AEC Regent	Roe H31/25R	
1946				
-	AAK224	Bedford WTL	Duple C26R	Ex.F.Garside new 1935. Not operated
1947				
217-26	ACP401-10	AEC Regent III	Park Royal H30/26R	217-8 to Corporation 1954
1948				
213-6	ACP627-30	AEC Regent III	Roe H31/25R	214 to driver trainer 1959
227-9	ACP411-3	AEC Regent III	Park Royal H30/26R	
230-4	ACP795-9	AEC Regent III	Park Royal H30/26R	
235-44	AJX361-70	AEC Regent III	Park Royal H30/26R	
1949				
245-50	AJX371-6	AEC Regent III	Park Royal H30/26R	

251-62	AJX841-52	AEC Regal III	Roe B32R	251/6-9/61/2 rebuilt to B33F 1953/4
263-9	BCP538-44	AEC Regal III	Roe B32R	263-9 rebuilt to B33F 1953/4. 269 to Corporation 1964 then back to JOC1964.

1950

270-83	BCP664-77	AEC Regent III	Park Royal H30/26R	

1954

284-93	DCP843-52	Daimler CVG6	MCCW H33/26R	294/5 to Corporation 1968

1959

201-8	KCP10-7	Leyland PD3/4	MCCW H40/32F	To CJOC 1971. To WYPTE 1974

1960

211-8	LJX211-8	AEC Regent V	MCCW H40/32F	To CJOC 1971. 211/3/5/7/8 to WYPTE 1974
221-8	MCP221-8	Leyland PD2/37	MCCW H36/28F	To CJOC 1971. 221-4/6-8 to WYPTE 1974

1961

231	OCP231	Leyland L2	Weymann B34D	Rebuilt to B42F 1963. To CJOC 1971. To WYPTE 1974

1962

232-8	PJX232-8	Leyland L1	Weymann B42F	To CJOC 1971. To WYPTE 1974
241-8	PJX241-8	Leyland PD2/37	Weymann H36/28F	To CJOC 1971. To WYPTE 1974

1963

250-9	RJX250-9	Albion NS3AN	Weymann B31F	

1964

269-70	AJX269-70B	Leyland L2	Willowbrook DP43F	To CJOC 1971. To WYPTE 1974
420	LUA420	AEC Regent III	Roe H31/25R	Ex.Leeds City Transport new 1947
422	LUA916	AEC Regent III	Roe H31/25R	Ex.Leeds City Transport new 1947
423	LUA423	AEC Regent III	Roe H31/25R	Ex.Leeds City Transport new 1947

1965

200	MBY347	AEC Reliance	Park Royal C41C	Ex.Holloway Coaches new 1954. Rebodied Plaxton C43F 1967. To CJOC 1971. To WYPTE 1974
267	CJX275C	Leyland L2	Willowbrook DP41F	To CJOC 1971. To WYPTE 1974
278-9	CCP523-4C	Leyland PD2/37	Roe H37/28F	To CJOC 1971. To WYPTE 1974
280-8	CJX320-8C	Leyland PD2/37	Weymann H36/28F	To CJOC 1971. To WYPTE 1974

1966

249-50	ECP949-50D	AEC Reliance	Pennine B39F	To CJOC 1971. To WYPTE 1974
253-4	ECP953-4D	AEC Reliance	Pennine B39F	To CJOC 1971. To WYPTE 1974
260	TGJ484	AEC Reliance	Burlingham C41F	Ex.A.Timpson new 1957. Rebodied Plaxton C43F 1967. To CJOC 1971. To WYPTE 1974
261	NRK350	AEC Reliance	Park Royal C41C	Ex.A.Timpson new 1955. Rebodied Plaxton C43F 1968. To CJOC 1971. To WYPTE 1974
262	PXO974	AEC Reliance	Park Royal C41C	Ex.A.Timpson new 1955. Rebodied Plaxton C43F 1968. To CJOC !971. To WYPTE 1974
263	TGJ485	AEC Rekiance	Burlingham C41F	Ex.A.Timpson new 1957
264	TGJ485	AEC Reliance	Burlingham C41F	Ex.A.Timpson new 1957
265-6	EJX65-6D	AEC Reliance	Willowbrook DP41F	To CJOC 1971. To WYPTE 1974
268	DJX143D	Leyland L2	Willowbrook DP41F	To CJOC 1971. To WYPTE 1974
289	CJX329C	Leyland PD2/37	Weymann H36/28F	To CJOC 1971. To WYPTE 1974

1967

251-2	ECP951-2D	AEC Reliance	Pennine B39F	To CJOC 1971. To WYPTE 1974
255	ECP955D	AEC Reliance	Pennine B39F	To CJOC 1971. To WYPTE 1974
300-4	FCP300-4E	Dennis Loline	NCME H41/33F	

1968

200	ODK770	AEC Reliance	Burlingham C41F	Ex.Streamline Taxi new 1956
262-4	JCP322-4F	AEC Reliance	Willowbrook DP41F	To CJOC 1971. To WYPTE 1974
290-1	JJX597-8G	Daimler CRG6LX	NCME H43/31F	290 to CJOC 1971 and to WYPTE 1974

1969

273-5	KCP873-5G	AEC Reliance	Plaxton C43F	To CJOC 1971. To WYPTE 1974
276-7	KCP876-7G	AEC Reloance	Plaxton DP43F	To CJOC 1971. To WYPTE 1974

1970

291	LJX403H	Daimler CRG6LX	NCME H43/31F	To CJOC 1971. To WYPTE 1974
292	LJX402H	Daimler CRG6LX	NCME H43/31F	To CJOC 1971. To WYPTE 1974
315-7	MJX15-7J	Seddon RU	Plaxton DP45F	To CJOC 1971. To WYPTE 1974

1971

260-1	OJX60-1K	AEC Reliance	Plaxton DP45F	To CJOC 1971. To WYPTE 1974
271-2	NJX854-5J	AEC Reliance	Plaxton C43F	To CJOC 1971. To WYPTE 1974
294	DJX351D	Daimler CRG6LX	NCME H43/31F	Ex.Yorkshire Woollen new 1966. To CJOC 1971. To WYPTE 1974
305-7	5075-7W	Leyland L1	Burlingham DP41F	Ex.Hebble new 1960. To CJOC 1971
308-9	5878-9W	Leyland L1	Burlingham DP41F	Ex.Yorkshire Woollen new 1960. To CJOC 1971
310	AJX410B	AEC Regent V	Weymann H40/30F	Ex.Hebble new 1964. To CJOC 1971. To WYPTE 1974
313	ALX409B	AEC Regent V	Weymann H40/30F	Ex.Hebble new 1964. To CJOC 1971. To WYPTE 1974
314	NCP414	AEC Regent V	MCCW H39/42F	Ex.Hebble new 1960. To CJOC 1971
318-9	NCP382-3	AEC Reliance	Park Royal B43F	Ex.Hebble new 1961. To CJOC 1971
320	BJX134C	AEC Reliance	Park Royal DP39F	Ex.Hebble new 1965. To CJOC 1971. To WYPTE 1974
358-9	NHE9-10F	Leyland PSU4B/4R	Marshall B45F	Ex.Yorkshire Traction new 1968. To CJOC 1971. To WYPTE 1974

CALDERDALE JOINT OMNIBUS COMMITTEE

Fleet No.	Reg'n No.	Chassis	Body	Notes
1971				
321-3	1880-2WA	Leyland L2	ECW C41F	Ex.Todmorden JOC new 1961. 323 to WYPTE 1974
324-5	NWW88-9E	Leyland L1	Willowbrook B43F	Ex.Todmorden JOC new 1967. To WYPTE 1974
326-7	NWW90-1E	Leyland L1	Willowbrook DP43F	Ex.Todmorden JOC new 1967. To WYPTE 1974
328-9	BWU688-9H	Leyland L1	Pennine DP43F	Ex.Todmorden JOC new 1969. To WYPTE 1974
330-3	BWU690-3H	Leyland PSU4A/2R	Pennine B43F	Ex.Todmorden JOC new 1969. To WYPTE 1974
334	634WY	Leyland L1	East Lancs B44F	Ex.Todmorden JOC new 1961. To WYPTE 1974
335-6	520-1BWT	Leyland L1	East Lancs B44F	Ex.Todmorden JOC new 1962. To WYPTE 1974
337-8	572-3EYG	Leyland L1	East Lancs B44F	Ex.Todmorden JOC new 1964. To WYPTE 1974
339	URR355	Leyland PSUC1/1	MCCW B44F	Ex.Todmorden JOC new 1956
340	YAL366	Leyland PSUC1/1	MCCW B44F	Ex.Todmorden JOC new 1958
351	HWY36	Leyland PD2/1	Leyland L27/26R	Ex.Todmorden JOC new 1950
352	JWY824	Leyland PD2/1	Leyland L27/16R	Ex.Todmorden JOC new 1950

353-4	KWX12/4	Leyland PD2/12	Leyland L27/26R	Ex.Todmorden JOC new 1951
355-7	KWX17-9	Leyland PD2/12	Leyland L27/26R	Ex.Todmorden JOC new 1951. 355/6 to WYPTE 1974
358	NHE8F	Leyland PSU4/4R	Marshall B45F	Ex.Yorkshire Traction new 1968. To WYPTE 1974
1972				
295-6	RCP282-3K	Daimler CRG6LX	NCME H43/31F	To WYPTE 1974
297-301	RCP277-81K	Daimler CRG6LX	NCME H43/31F	To WYPTE 1974
302-6	RCP332-6K	Daimler CRG6LX	NCME H43/31F	To WYPTE 1974
361/2	VKR472/9	AEC Regent V	Park Royal H33/26RD	Ex.Maidstone & District new 1956
363-4	VKR36-7	AEC Regent V	Park Royal L30/26RD	Ex.Maidstone & District new 1956
1973				
309-11	VCP839-41M	Daimler CRG6LX	NCME H43/31F	To WYPTE 1974
1974				
307-8	VCP837-8M	Daimler CRG6LX	NCME H43/31F	To WYPTE 1974

All the vehicles are shown with their original fleet numbers. Many were subsequently renumbered within their respective fleets or when exchanged between the Corporation and Joint Omnibus Committees. Those passing to West Yorkshire PTE in 1974 had 3000 added to their existing fleet numbers.

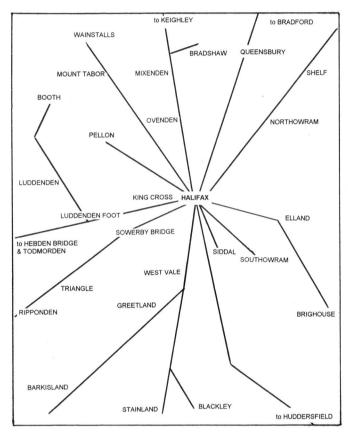

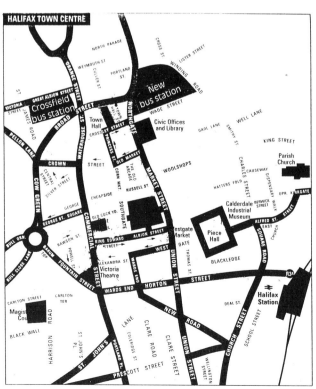

FRONT COVER :

Upper left : **Still wearing West Yorkshire PTE livery but sporting Yorkshire Rider fleet names, Roe-bodied Leyland Atlantean 6176 (GWR176T) was on loan to Halifax district when caught leaving Bradford Transport Interchange in 1987.**   *K.A.Jenkinson*

Centre left : **NCME-bodied Fleetline 7204 (PTD642S) seen near King Cross, Halifax in October 1998 painted in First Calderline livery has been purchased twice from GM Buses.**   *K.A.Jenkinson*

Lower left : **First Calderline low-floor Plaxton Pointer 2-bodied Dennis Dart SLF 3325 (R341HYG) shows off its FirstGroup corporate livery as it passes through Illingworth on a journey to Halifax in October 1998.**   *K.A.Jenkinson*

Right : **Halifax Corporation Roe-bodied Daimler CVG6 (DCP835) looks resplendent in the undertaking's traditional livery as it returns to Halifax from Southowram on route 30, its crew having forgotten to change its destination display.**   *N.Harris*

BACK COVER :

Top left : **2507 (NAK507H), one of the Marshall-bodied Leyland Panthers transferred to Metro Calderdale from Bradford is seen in Metrobus livery at Northowram on route 577.**   *J.Sharp*

Upper centre left : **Painted in West Yorkshire PTE's Gold Rider coaching livery, Plaxton Paramount 3200-bodied Leyland Tiger 1616 (F616XWY) prepares to leave Halifax bus station at the start of its journey to Huddersfield on limited stop service X37.**   *K.A.Jenkinson*

Lower centre left : **Heading through the Calder Valley on its way to Halifax and sporting Yorkshire Rider Todmorden fleet names is 5191 (FUM495Y), an ECW-bodied Leyland Olympian acquired from West Yorkshire Road Car Co. in 1990.**   *K.A.Jenkinson*

Bottom left : **Repainted in the old Halifax Joint Omnibus Committee coach livery, CalderLine Plaxton-bodied Leyland Tiger 1606 (WSV410, originally HUA606Y) approaches Salterhebble in June 1996 after completing a private hire duty.**   *K.A.Jenkinson*

Top right : **7236 (TWH691T), an NCME-bodied Fleetline acquired from GM Buses in 1988 is seen here enroute to Wainstalls in June 1996 still wearing its Yorkshire Rider livery but sporting CalderLine fleet names.**   *K.A.Jenkinson*

Upper centre right : **Painted in Calderline's new livery and adorned with FirstBus logos and the short-lived fleet name style which used an upper case 'L', Plaxton Beaver-bodied Mercedes Benz 709D 2251 ((M251VWU) leaves Halifax bus station on a journey to Washer Lane.** *K.A.Jenkinson*

Lower centre right : **All the new full-size buses taken into stock by First Calderline are painted in FirstGroup's corporate livery as illustrated by Alexander Royale-bodied Volvo Olympian 5639 (R639HYG) seen at Queensbury operating Gold Service 576 from Bradford to Halifax.**   *K.A.Jenkinson*

Bottom right : **Proving that the old Halifax livery of orange, green & cream is not dead, independent Halifax Joint Committee has adopted these colours for its four-vehicle fleet. Ex.London Buses Routemaster 214CLT wearing the pre-war scheme with grey roof is seen resting in Halifax bus station in October 1998 prior to taking up its next duty on the 44A service to Sowerby.**   *K.A.Jenkinson*